A PRIMER OF
OPERANT CONDITIONING

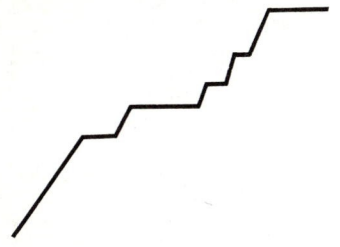

A PRIMER OF
OPERANT CONDITIONING

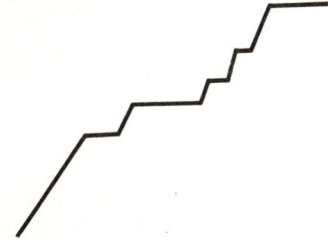

G. S. REYNOLDS
University of California, San Diego

SCOTT, FORESMAN AND COMPANY

Library of Congress Catalog Card No. 68-11515.
Copyright © 1968 by Scott, Foresman and Company, Glenview, Illinois 60025.
All rights reserved. Printed in the United States of America.
Regional offices of Scott, Foresman and Company are located in Atlanta,
Dallas, Glenview, Palo Alto, and Oakland, N.J.

Preface

This primer presents a concise but detailed account of the theory and principles of operant conditioning. It is derived largely from the work of B. F. Skinner and his first- and second-generation intellectual descendants, whose collective efforts have won for operant conditioning a deserved place among the forerunners of current psychological approaches.

No branch of psychology is today untouched by the concepts of operant conditioning. Most obviously, experimental studies of learning and performance have been vastly facilitated by Skinner's box; but the other traditional fields of motivation, emotion, language, and thinking owe as great a debt, although it is as yet largely unrecognized and unpaid. Even students of perception, that obdurately most mental of the disciplines, have gained insight from the proper formulation of the discriminative functions of a stimulus. Outside the psychologist's laboratory, education and training have been offered hope of revolution by programed instruction, a direct outgrowth of operant principles. Developmental theorists are increasingly grounding their concepts in findings from operant research. Ethologists also have benefited from the discovery that the consequences of even innate behavior patterns contribute to the form and future fate of such patterns. And the psychotherapeutic process has undergone radical reappraisal in the light of the insistence of operant conditioning that actual changes in the patient's behavior are the only valid index of cure or improvement. This basic approach to mental illness has, in fact, crystallized into a successful behavioral therapy.

Yet despite the ubiquity, influence, and impact of operant principles, many of them are still misunderstood. One purpose of this primer is to help dissolve these misunderstandings. This purpose will be fulfilled if the theorist comes to a greater appreciation of the richness of the concepts of operant conditioning, if the educator finds here a key to a surer feel for the behavior he hopes to augment, if the psychologist, practiced or apprenticed, finds the courage and the justification to speak of learning instead only of learning theory, and if the student is intrigued by the barely tapped potentialities of the experimental analysis of behavior.

The topics in this primer have been taken up in a logical order, and as aids to the student, there are numerous cross references between chapters as well as a complete index. The theoretical creed and experimental methods are presented first, followed by chapters on the basic facts of acquisition (including shaping) and extinction; the functions of a discriminative stimulus in discrimination, generalization, and secondary, or conditioned, reinforcement; and the complexities of the notion of contingency. There follows a thorough, though concise, exposition and analysis of schedules of reinforcement and the performances they maintain. Pavlov's respondent conditioning is introduced at length just before the treatment of avoidance, escape, and punishment, since it is only at this point that it is really needed. The necessary coextensiveness of operant and respondent conditioning with both positive and negative reinforcement is explained and emphasized. The primer ends with a discussion of emotion and motivation. In this section, it has proved feasible to introduce the approach of operant conditioning to the analysis of the verbal behaviors of gesture and language. For those whose curiosity is aroused, additional information on operant conditioning can be obtained from the list of supplementary readings at the end of the text.

I would like to acknowledge the editorial assistance of Mrs. Marguerite Clark, Mrs. Kay Mueller, and Mrs. Maud Benjamin of the Scott, Foresman staff, and especially that of A. C. Catania. I am grateful to my teachers, R. L. Solomon and R. J. Herrnstein, for initially arousing my interest in experiment and analysis and to G. v. Békésy for suggesting that I write down the principles of this field in order to see if the terms and concepts maintain in the complex the meanings they were given in the simple. Answering this question is a highly recommended exercise for the serious reader.

G. S. R.
Del Mar
7 June 1967

Contents

one

Introduction to the experimental analysis of behavior

WHAT IS OPERANT CONDITIONING?

Operant conditioning is an experimental science of behavior. Strictly speaking, the term *operant conditioning* refers to a process in which the frequency of occurrence of a bit of behavior is modified by the consequences of the behavior. Over the years, however, operant conditioning has come to refer to an entire approach to psychological science. This approach is characterized in general by a deterministic and experimental analysis of behavior. It is also characterized by a concentration on the study of operant or instrumental behavior, although not to the exclusion of the study of instinctive and reflexive behavior.

As an approach to the study of behavior, operant conditioning consists of a series of assumptions about behavior and its environment; a set of definitions which can be used in the objective, scientific description of behavior and its environment; a group of techniques and procedures for the experimental study of behavior in the laboratory; and a large body of facts and principles which have been demonstrated by experiment.

Operant conditioning is concerned with the relationship between the behavior of organisms and their environment. Research in operant conditioning gathers knowledge about behavior from the experimental study of the effects on behavior of systematic changes in the surrounding environment. Operant conditioning attempts to understand behavior by gaining knowledge of the factors that modify behavior. As an objective science, it is restricted to the study of factors that can be observed, measured, and reproduced. The science of operant conditioning has accumulated an enormous body of knowledge and has taken great strides toward a complete answer to the question: What makes organisms behave as they do?

The psychologists who use this approach differ greatly in their degree of commitment to the principles of operant conditioning. At one extreme of commitment are those who accept only the experimental techniques because they are convenient methods for studying behavior. At the other extreme are those who accept, at present partly on faith, the beliefs and findings of operant conditioning as being truly descriptive of behavior and as guides to the conduct of their personal lives.

This primer presents, concisely but as completely as possible, the concepts, methods, and findings of operant conditioning. This first chapter will concentrate on basic assumptions underlying the science and on definitions of fundamental concepts.

THE EXPLANATION OF BEHAVIOR

What makes organisms behave as they do? This question is notably subject to insufficient and incomplete answers. A man is said to go to the store because he "wants" a certain article that is sold at the store. A child is said to steal because his "superego" has failed to operate. A dog is said to perform tricks because it "needs" affection. Explanations such as these—which are stated in terms of the will, hypothetical divisions of an organism's mental apparatus, or the presumed needs of an organism—are not acceptable in operant conditioning because they do not specify the actual environmental conditions under which the behavior will reliably occur. Instead, they offer reasons which themselves require explanation. Thus, it is still necessary to determine the conditions under which the man will want to go, the child's superego will fail, or the dog's needs will be expressed in tricks.

In operant conditioning an adequate explanation of behavior is one that specifies the actual conditions which reliably produce the behavior to be explained. Statements about the causes of behavior are accepted as valid only when they specify what can actually be done under given circumstances to produce that behavior. The behavior is understood only when it can be shown experimentally that under these circumstances, specified changes in the environment do actually result in the behavior. Because explanation in operant conditioning requires the experimental production and manipulation of behavior, the actual control of behavior becomes an essential part of the process of explanation. In operant research, to understand behavior is to control it, and vice versa.

The Environmental Determinants of Behavior

The specification of the environmental conditions under which behavior will reliably occur is not so difficult as it might seem. In fact, the science of operant conditioning has already made much progress in demonstrating how behavior can be controlled by the environment and how the environment can be described objectively and in detail.

There are two kinds of environmental determinants of behavior: the contemporary and the historical. The behavior of an organism at any one moment is determined not only by the currently acting, contemporary environment but also by the organism's previous experience with these, or similar, environmental conditions. Thus, a man brakes his car to a stop at an intersection not only because there is a red light but also because of his previous experiences with red lights. A child stops talking when told not only because he is told to stop but also because of his previous experiences with the consequences of not obeying. A dog runs to the kitchen when his food is taken from the shelf not only because of the noise of the moving can but also because of its previous experiences with such noises.

Operant conditioning is concerned with the experimental analysis of both kinds of determinants of behavior. In dealing with contemporary causes, it tries to determine, through observation and experiment, the particular environmental event which is responsible for the behavior. The man brakes only when the light is red, not when it is green; and he continues his journey when the light changes from red to green. The red light is the environmental condition which brings about the specific behavior of braking. By experimentally manipulating the contemporary conditions of which the behavior is a function, we can control the man's behavior. Thus, if we change the light at the corner to red, the man brakes; if we let it continue to be green, he does not.

Historical determinants of behavior are more difficult to specify, if only because they invariably involve several experiences over a period of time. However, the specification of historical determinants can be as exact as the specification of contemporary determinants. In the case of the dog's running to the kitchen, we might suppose that the noise of the can resulted in the running because of the dog's previous experience. Specifically, we may speculate that the running occurs after the noise because this behavior has previously been followed by food from the can. But this explanation, unless developed further, is little better than saying that the dog runs because it wants the food. We have not yet demonstrated exactly what historical experiences are necessary for the occurrence of the behavior.

The fact that past experience with the sequence noise-running-food is in part responsible for the current behavior can be established experimentally by either of two possible methods. One is to change the dog's experience and see if this brings about a change in its behavior. Since the dog's historical experience is in the past, it cannot be changed directly; but it is possible to create a new history of experience for the dog by exposing it to new and different experiences for several weeks. For example, suppose that from now on a whistle always announces the dog's meals and the noise of the can does not. In practice, this involves both taking the can down noisily from the shelf and not feeding the dog, even though it comes to the kitchen, and taking the can down quietly and whistling when the dog is to be fed. If, as we have supposed, the dog's previous experiences of receiving food when it ran to the kitchen following the noise from the can were responsible for its running, the dog should run to the kitchen when we whistle and no longer run when it hears the noise of the can. Through experience, the whistle comes to be the environmental event after which running to the kitchen is followed by food, and the noise of the can becomes an event after which running is not followed by food. If the dog's behavior does not change in our experiment, then we have made an incorrect supposition about the historical determinants of its behavior.

A second method of studying historical determinants of behavior is to create the same history of previous experiences in another, similar organism. If our assumptions are correct, any other dog should also run at the noise of the can if running to the kitchen after the noise has resulted in food in that dog's experience. As both of these methods indicate, operant conditioning rejects mere plausible speculations about the causes of behavior and aims at direct experimental demonstration of the contemporary and historical determinants of behavior.

Summary Statement

Experimental analyses such as those described above have led to the conclusion summarized in this statement: The characteristics of behavior and its probability of occurrence are determined by the environmental conditions and events which precede and accompany the behavior, by the environmental events which change after or as a consequence of the behavior, and by the organism's previous experience with the environment. It is within the context of this statement that operant conditioning studies behavior.

Behavior in this formulation refers to everything that organisms do. Most behavior, such as the dog's running to the kitchen, can be seen. Some behavior, such as speaking, may only be heard. Other behavior, such as thinking, is ordinarily accessible only to the organism that does the behaving. The *environment* in this formulation includes everything that has an effect on the organism, whether or not that effect is immediate. The environment thus includes the organism's own behavior, since one of the determinants of current behavior may be the behavior which preceded it. The *consequences* of behavior are simply the environmental events which follow the behavior closely in time. In our previous example, the food was a consequence of the dog's running to the kitchen.

In operant conditioning, the emphasis is placed on the *probability* that behavior will occur. In our example, we tacitly assumed that the dog always ran at the noise and, later, that it always ran at the whistle; that is to say, we assumed that the probability of running was 1.0. Because such perfection is not always the case with behavior, we usually speak of the probability that the behavior will occur under given circumstances. If the dog ran only half the time when we whistled, the probability of running would be 0.5. Thus one meaning of *probability* is the frequency of occurrence of the behavior relative to the frequency of occurrence of certain environmental conditions.

Probability may also be understood in the sense of absolute frequency or rate of occurrence. Behavior which occurs more frequently now than it did formerly is more probable now than formerly. As we shall see in Chapter 3, other interesting characteristics of behavior besides its rate of occurrence are determined by the environment and by the consequences of the behavior. However, since the primary goal of operant conditioning is to predict and manipulate the occurrence of a given behavior under a given set of environmental conditions, one of its major concerns is the rate, or probability, of occurrence of the behavior under those conditions.

THE BASIC CONCEPTS OF BEHAVIOR

Any experimental science relies on description as well as on experiment. The descriptive system of a science breaks its subject matter down into elements that can be clearly defined and communicated. The basic concepts of operant conditioning describe behavior and the environment reliably and precisely. As a result, all members of the scientific community interested in behavior and its control are able to understand the descriptions and to reproduce the measurements of behavior and the environment that are the basis of the science.

Stimuli and Responses

In operant conditioning, we think of behavior as segmented into units called *responses.* We think of the environment as segmented into units called *stimuli.* Unfortunately, both terms are somewhat misleading, because they do not refer in operant conditioning to what their ordinary meanings suggest. Responses, the units of behavior, need not be "replies" to the environment. Indeed, we shall see that one of the most fundamental concepts of operant conditioning is that most behavior is not necessarily forced from the organism by the environment. Nor do stimuli necessarily incite the organism to action. In fact, it is fundamental in operant conditioning to approach the environment from an entirely opposite point of view. Thus, it is necessary to understand the more precise definitions of these terms as they are used in operant conditioning.

The responses composing behavior are separated into two classes: one class is called operant, or instrumental, responses; and the other is called respondent, or reflexive, responses. In operant conditioning, these two kinds of responses are called *operants* and *respondents.*

The environment is divided into several classes of stimuli. One class, the *eliciting stimuli,* is composed of environmental events which regularly precede responses. These stimuli elicit relatively fixed and stereotyped responses, the respondents mentioned above. A second class of stimuli, the *reinforcing stimuli,* or *reinforcers,* is composed of environmental events which follow responses. Reinforcing stimuli increase the frequency of the responses they follow; they increase the probability that these responses will reoccur in the future behavior of the organism. The responses which become more probable when they are followed by reinforcers are the operants mentioned above. Members of a third class of stimuli, called *discriminative stimuli,* precede and accompany operants but do not elicit them as the eliciting stimuli elicit respondents. Rather, the presence of particular discriminative stimuli increases the probability of those operants which have previously been reinforced in the presence of the same discriminative stimuli. Still another class of stimuli is composed of *neutral stimuli.* This class includes all those environmental events which at any particular time bring about no change at all in behavior, whether they precede, accompany, or follow responses.

These divisions of behavior and the environment are the fundamental concepts of the approach to the study of behavior called operant conditioning. They have grown out of the efforts of experimental psychologists to describe behavior and the environment in ways that will be scientifically useful. So far, we have presented them only in a skeletal form. What follows is a more detailed discussion of each of these concepts.

Eliciting Stimuli and Respondents

All organisms are provided by nature with reflexes, or innate inherited responses to certain environmental events. Generally, these responses provide automatic behavioral protection and sustenance for the animal from its earliest hours of contact with its environment. A thorn piercing a dog's paw automatically elicits flexion, which raises the leg. A bright light on the eye elicits constriction of the pupil. Vinegar in the mouth elicits secretion of the salivary glands. Stroking the palm of a child elicits grasping. A sudden loud noise elicits startling. In each of these reflexes, a stimulus elicits a response because of the inherited structure of the organism and not because the organism has had any specific previous experience with the stimulus. The same stimulus elicits the same response from all normal organisms of the same species (and, to be technically precise, of the same sex and age). As defined above, such a stimulus is called an *eliciting stimulus*, and the response, a *respondent*.

Two characteristics of respondents should be given special notice because they play a major part in separating respondents from operants. First, the frequency of occurrence of a respondent depends primarily on the frequency of occurrence of its eliciting stimulus. Respondents rarely occur spontaneously, in the absence of an eliciting stimulus. To increase or decrease the frequency of occurrence of a respondent, it is necessary only to increase or decrease the frequency of its eliciting stimulus. Second, the consequences of respondents— the environmental events which follow them—do not usually affect their frequency. A thorn thrust into the sole of the foot, for example, elicits flexion of the leg regardless of whether or not the thorn comes out of the foot as a result of the flexion.

RESPONDENT CONDITIONING

The respondent behavior of an organism changes very little, if at all, throughout the organism's life. Leg flexion elicited by a thorn in the foot of an old dog is essentially the same as flexion elicited from a young dog by the same stimulus. What does happen during the life of an organism is that new stimuli, previously ineffective, come to elicit respondents from the organism. This happens when a new stimulus occurs again and again at the same time as (or slightly before) an eliciting stimulus. Gradually the new stimulus comes to elicit a respondent similar to that originally produced only by the eliciting stimulus.

This process, whereby new stimuli gain the power to elicit respondents, is called *respondent conditioning*. The traditional example involves the conditioning of the respondent, salivation. At first, only food or acid actually placed in the mouth elicits salivation. But gradually, during the early life of an organism, the sight and smell of food also come to elicit salivation because they regularly precede and accompany the original eliciting stimulus, food in the mouth.

Respondents and respondent conditioning are discussed in detail in Chapter 8. For the present it should suffice to remember only two facts. First, respondents are innate behavior regularly elicited by specific stimuli which precede them and largely unaffected by stimuli which follow them. And, second, respondent conditioning involves the repeated presentation of a new stimulus along with a stimulus that already elicits a respondent. The new stimulus then acquires the power to elicit the respondent.

OPERANT CONDITIONING

Elicited respondents represent only a small proportion of the behavior of the higher organisms. The remaining behavior is operant. There is no environmental eliciting stimulus for operant behavior; it simply occurs. In the terminology of operant conditioning, operants are *emitted* by the organism. The dog walks, runs, and romps; the bird flies; the monkey swings from tree to tree; the human infant babbles vocally. In each case, the behavior occurs without any specific eliciting stimulus. The initial cause of operant behavior is within the organism itself. The organism simply uses its inherited muscular and skeletal structure in relation to the environment in which it finds itself. It is in the biological nature of organisms to emit operant behavior.

Reinforcing Stimuli and Operant Behavior

It is clear from observation that some operants occur more frequently than others and that the frequency with which a given operant occurs can change. Closer observation suggests that the frequency of occurrence of an operant is greatly influenced by the consequences of the operant. Whereas the frequency of respondent behavior is determined mainly by the frequency of its eliciting stimulus (the environmental event that precedes it), the frequency of operant behavior is primarily determined by its effect (the environmental event that follows it).

The effects or consequences of behavior may be either the appearance of an additional part of the environment or the disappearance of some part of the environment. If the appearance of a stimulus as a consequence of a response results in an increased probability that the response will reoccur in the future, the stimulus is called a *positive reinforcing stimulus,* or *positive reinforcer.* If the disappearance of a stimulus as a consequence of a response results in an increased probability that the response will reoccur in the future, the stimulus is called an *aversive stimulus,* or *negative reinforcer.*

A reinforcer is always defined in terms of its effects on the subsequent frequency of the response which immediately preceded it. A dog, for example, may one day open the door to its play area with a hard nudge of the forepaws. If this particular behavior occurs more frequently in the future, we call the opening of the door to the play area a *positive reinforcer.* Negative reinforcement, on the other hand, involves the disappearance of an aversive stimulus. Suppose that the dog manages to dislodge a tick from its paw by rubbing the paw down the side of a venetian blind. If in the future there is an increased tendency to rub the paw against the blind whenever a tick gets onto the paw, we call the presence of the tick an *aversive stimulus* and its removal a *negative reinforcer,* which reinforces the response of rubbing the paw on the blind.

Reinforcers are many and varied. Positive reinforcers, events which reinforce by their appearance, range from food and water to novel stimuli. Aversive stimuli, events which reinforce by their disappearance, range from discordant noise to life-threatening situations. In any case of reinforcement, an operant occurs, has an effect on the environment, and, because of the effect, occurs more frequently in the future.

Discriminative Stimuli and Stimulus Control

Most operants occur with a high frequency only under certain conditions. One rarely, if ever, recites the Gettysburg Address unless faced with an audience of listeners. The dog enters the kitchen infrequently except at the usual time for its meals. One rarely turns off a radio which shows no signs of being on. These are examples of the control of operant behavior by discriminative stimuli. In each case, the probability of the operant is high only in the presence of certain environmental events—the discriminative stimuli—and it is low under other conditions. In operant conditioning, the discriminative stimuli are said to *control* the operant response. The rule for the control of behavior by discriminative stimuli is that an operant will occur at a high frequency in the presence of the discriminative stimuli which in the past have accompanied the occurrence of the operant and have set the occasion for its reinforcement.

To bring an operant under the control of a discriminative stimulus, it is necessary to reinforce occurrences of the operant in the presence of the stimulus and not in the absence of the stimulus. This procedure was followed, for example, when the dog was trained to run to the kitchen at the sound of a whistle. The whistle was a discriminative stimulus in whose presence the operant, running, was reinforced with food, and the whistle came to control the running. As another example, suppose that we want the dog to sit on command and that it already sits frequently because sitting has been previously reinforced with small pieces of sugar. To bring the operant, sitting, under the control of the discriminative stimulus, "Sit," we give a lump of sugar to the dog whenever we command "Sit" and the dog does, in fact, sit. At the same time, we do not reinforce sitting unless it is done on command. Gradually, the dog comes to sit promptly when told to sit and rarely does so otherwise. In operant conditioning, we say that the (operant) response of sitting has been brought under the control of the discriminative stimulus, "Sit," by reinforcing the response in the presence of the stimulus.

The relation beween a discriminative stimulus and an operant is fundamentally different from the relation between an eliciting stimulus and a respondent. The discriminative stimulus controls the operant because the operant has been reinforced in its presence, not because of the inherited structure of the organism. There is nothing special about the stimulus, "Sit," which destines it for control over the response of sitting. Nor is there anything special about the operant, sitting, which fits it for control by the discriminative stimulus, "Sit." We can just as easily train a dog to sit when we say "Stand" and to stand when we say "Sit," simply by reinforcing the appropriate response when the appropriate command has been given. This is not the case, however, with the fixed eliciting relationship between food in the mouth and salivation, for example. The operant relation between a discriminative stimulus and an operant response is established and determined only by whether or not the operant is reinforced in the presence of the discriminative stimulus. The stimulus which precedes the response in the operant case is arbitrary. The control of behavior by discriminative stimuli is discussed further in Chapter 4.

Conditioned Reinforcers

Some stimuli, such as food and water, are able to reinforce behavior without the organism's having any particular previous experience with them. These stimuli are called *primary*, or *unconditioned, reinforcers*. Other stimuli, however, acquire the power to reinforce behavior during the lifetime and through the experience of the organism. These stimuli are called *secondary*, or *conditioned, reinforcers*.

Conditioned reinforcers acquire the power to reinforce operants through a procedure which is similar to that resulting in respondent conditioning. When a new stimulus is repeatedly presented to an organism at the same time as or just prior to another stimulus which already has the power to reinforce behavior, the new stimulus may itself acquire the power to reinforce behavior. If so, it becomes a conditioned reinforcer, and behavior which precedes it becomes more probable in the future. Notice that although both discriminative stimuli and conditioned reinforcers share the acquired power to increase the probability of a response, discriminative stimuli precede or accompany the occurrence of the behavior while conditioned reinforcers follow behavior as a consequence, just as do primary reinforcers.

One classic example of conditioned reinforcement involves the establishment of poker chips as reinforcers of a chimpanzee's behavior. The chimp's behavior may initially be reinforced by grapes, which it eats. If the chimp is repeatedly given a chance to exchange poker chips for grapes, the poker chips themselves become reinforcers. The poker chips can then be used to reinforce the chimp's behavior. The chimp will even operate a vending machine which dispenses poker chips. Because they have been exchanged for grapes, the poker chips have become conditioned reinforcers.

Instances of conditioned reinforcement involve orderly sequences of stimuli and responses, which in operant conditioning are called *chains*. In our example, the chimp operates the vending machine, receives a poker chip, exchanges the poker chip for a grape, and eats the grape. The response, operating the machine, is made in the presence of the discriminative stimuli afforded by the vending machine and is reinforced by a conditioned reinforcer, the appearance of the poker chip. The poker chip is also a discriminative stimulus (the second one in the chain), in whose presence the response of exchanging is reinforced by the appearance of the grape, another conditioned reinforcer. The grape is the third discriminative stimulus in the chain. In its presence, the response, popping it into the mouth, is reinforced by the primary reinforcing stimuli afforded by the eating of the grape. The general formula for chains is that one response leads to a stimulus in whose presence another response leads to another stimulus. Each stimulus functions both as a conditioned reinforcer, when it reinforces the response which precedes it, and as a discriminative stimulus, when it occasions another response in its presence. Chains are thus orderly sequences of stimuli and responses held together by stimuli which function both as conditioned reinforcers and as discriminative stimuli. Conditioned reinforcement and the nature of chains are discussed further in Chapter 5.

So far, we have delineated the broad field of operant conditioning as an approach to the study of behavior, and we have defined the basic elements of stimuli and responses and the concepts of conditioning and reinforcement. Next, in Chapter 2, we will examine the nature and practice of research in operant conditioning.

two

Research in
operant conditioning

WHAT IS RESEARCH?

Research is the cornerstone of an experimental science. Both the certainty of the conclusions and the rapidity of the progress of an experimental science depend intimately and ultimately on its research. As its root meaning ("to search again") implies, most research either results in a rediscovery, and hence a confirmation, of already known facts and principles or represents another painstaking attempt to answer a formerly unanswered question in an objective and repeatable fashion. But research also means the search for and the discovery of formerly misunderstood or unconceived principles and facts. Research is, in practice, a two-pronged fork with one tine in the past and the other in the future. An experiment attempts to confirm or deny what is already believed to be true and at the same time to go beyond existing knowledge toward either a more comprehensive body of facts or, if possible, toward a general principle around which all the known and verifiable facts about a subject may cluster in a logical, predictable, and sensible whole.

THE GOAL OF RESEARCH

The ultimate goal of research is always a general principle. Rarely, however, does a single experiment directly establish a general principle. A single experiment is concerned with the relation between a specific *independent variable,* which is manipulated by the experimenter, and a specific *dependent variable,* which changes as a result of changes in the independent variable. Each of such relations, established repeatedly in laboratories around the world, contributes to the formulation of the general principle. For example, several hundred experiments have shown that variations in a stimulus in whose presence a response has been reinforced (the independent variable) produce in an organism a decreased tendency to emit the response (the dependent variable). If responding has been reinforced in the presence of a bright light, the organism will respond less and less as the light becomes dimmer and dimmer. If responding has been reinforced in the presence of a green light, the organism will respond less in the presence of either a yellow or blue light. Many other experiments have had similar results. Together, they all figure in the formulation of the principle of stimulus generalization (to be discussed in Chapter 4). No single piece of research is sufficient to formulate a general principle; rather, each experiment contributes, either by repeating and verifying what is believed or by extending the generality of the principle.

In operant conditioning, research relates changes in the environment (the independent variable) to changes in behavior (the dependent variable). The experiments of operant conditioning arrange for the occurrence of specific environmental events and changes in them and for the measurement of behavior and its changes as a function of the changes in the environment. Each particular relation established between the environment and an organism's behavior helps form the basis for what operant experimenters hope will be a general principle concerning the prediction and control—that is to say, the understanding—of behavior.

EXPERIMENTAL ANALYSIS AND INDIVIDUAL ORGANISMS

Two characteristics distinguish the operant approach to research from other psychological approaches. In order to be accepted into the group of established facts, a given relation between the environment and behavior must meet two criteria. First and primarily, it must be unequivocally demonstrated for every organism in the experiment. And second, it must be based on an actual experimental analysis of behavior.

To require that experimental conditions produce the same effects on each and every subject in the experiment is a stringent requirement for any science. Many sciences, including most kinds of psychological science, are able and willing to settle for average effects. A relation is considered to be established if the measurements of the dependent variable for one group of subjects differ on the average from the average of the measurements for another group of subjects which was treated differently in the experiment. In operant research, however, effects that are defined only by the averages of groups of organisms are not acceptable. The effect of a change in the independent variable of the environment is accepted as valid only if it in fact brings about the same change in the behavior of every single organism subjected to the change. It is not enough that the change in the environmental conditions bring about an effect on the average; it is absolutely necessary that the change in the environment change the behavior of every organism in the same way.

Of course, this does not always happen. Organisms differ, and they differ for different reasons. When the environmental changes arranged by the experiment result in different changes in the behavior of the individual subjects, the second hallmark of operant research — the experimental analysis of behavior — comes into prominence. The experimental analysis of behavior means nothing more than what we have emphasized in the first chapter: that research in operant conditioning strives to find the exact, real, and specifiable changes in the environment that actually do bring about exact, real, and specifiable changes in the behavior of organisms. When organisms differ, experimental analysis attempts to demonstrate exactly what factors in the history or present environment of each organism are responsible for the difference. Experimental analysis is hard, time-consuming work; but it pays off in knowledge that can be applied with certainty to the prediction and control of the behavior of individual organisms.

THE EXPERIMENTAL ORGANISMS

Research in operant conditioning requires detailed, extensive, and precise control over the environment of the subjects in an experiment — which is why human beings cannot ordinarily be used as subjects. For the sake of standardization and convenience, one of three animals is usually used: the pigeon, the rat, or the monkey. These animals are often raised specifically for research purposes. A great deal is usually known about their environment since birth, and when they are brought to the laboratory of the operant experimenter, their environment is also highly controlled.

Human beings, especially persons institutionalized for mental illness, have also recently been used as experimental subjects. Naturally, their environment cannot be controlled as precisely as that of the usual experimental animals, but researchers are as rigorous as possible. Research with these institutionalized human beings has been quite successful; many people whose difficulties had not yielded to traditional methods of treatment have been helped by the techniques of operant conditioning.

THE EXPERIMENTAL APPARATUS

The exact environmental control required by research in operant conditioning has produced a special technology that is particularly suited to the approach to behavior and the environment which we have described as characteristic of operant conditioning. The apparatus and recording equipment are specially suited to the problems involved in the study of operant behavior. Because the organisms that are studied differ in their sensory and behavioral propensities, the details of the apparatus are different for each organism. The basic features of each, however, are the same.

During each daily experimental session of a few hours, the organism under study in a particular experiment is housed in an isolated cubicle, called an *experimental chamber.* Isolation is essential in order to minimize the contribution to the results of the experiment of outside, extraneous influences. The experimental chamber is usually light-tight and sound-attenuating and generally has a loudspeaker which presents a flat hissing sound to drown out potentially disturbing noises from the outside. The chamber is ventilated because of the subject's relatively long daily stay in it. Electrical connections from the chamber to automatic programing and recording equipment make possible the remote control and remote recording of the environmental and behavioral events within the chamber. Not even the experimenter comes into direct contact with the subject during the experiment.

Inside the chamber there is provision for the delivery of a reinforcer, such as food or water. A variety of other stimuli can also be provided, all under remote control. The stimuli are usually auditory or spatial for rats and visual for pigeons, monkeys, and men. Finally, each chamber contains one or more devices which define the operant responses to be studied.

Definition of Operant Responses

We said in the previous chapter that behavior is divided into units called *responses,* which are themselves divided into two types, operant and respondent. For experimental purposes, we need a specific, empirical definition of an operant response. How can we recognize a response when one is made? And how can we count the number of responses that occur per minute?

An operant response is defined in terms of its effect on the environment. An *operant* is a class of behaviors all of which change the environment in the same way. The response most commonly used in operant conditioning is the closing of a switch resembling a telegraph key, although any other objective effect on the environment might be chosen. Each closure of the switch counts as one occurrence of the response, regardless of the particular behavior that brought it about. The behavior composing the operant may be any of a large variety: the animal may close the switch by using its foot, nose, beak, head, or any part of its body in any sort of movement. These variations in the actual behavior are of no concern in defining the response. Regardless of the particular behavior involved at any one time, the effect, closing the switch, is still counted as one response.

By this definition, operant responses are rendered recognizable and countable. The response may be described exactly in terms of the switch—its location in the animal's environment, its physical characteristics (usually it is some kind of a lever), the amount of force that must be exerted on it in order to bring about closure, and the distance which it must move in order to close. The actual occurrence of a response and the number of times the animal responds in a given period of time are obtained simply by observing the switch and counting the number of times it operates. We will be further concerned with the definition of the operant response and its measurement in Chapter 3.

Operant Apparatus for the Pigeon

The specialized apparatus for the study of the pigeon's operant behavior appears in Figure 2.1, along with its associated experimental equipment. The important features of the apparatus can be seen in the picture. A close-up of the interior of the experimental chamber appears in Figure 2.2. Notice the walls and cover, which insulate the chamber against light and sound; the loudspeaker in the upper left corner of the front wall, for presenting auditory stimuli; and the diffuse illumination provided to the inside of the chamber through the window in the upper right corner of the front wall.

Provision has been made on the front wall of the chamber for the recording of responses and for the presentation of the reinforcer and various discriminative stimuli. The operant is defined by means of the round key in the upper center of the wall. The key is a plastic lever

Figure 2.1 The operant conditioning apparatus used with the pigeon, including the experimental chamber and programing and recording equipment on the relay rack. *Courtesy of the Grason-Stadler Company, Inc.*

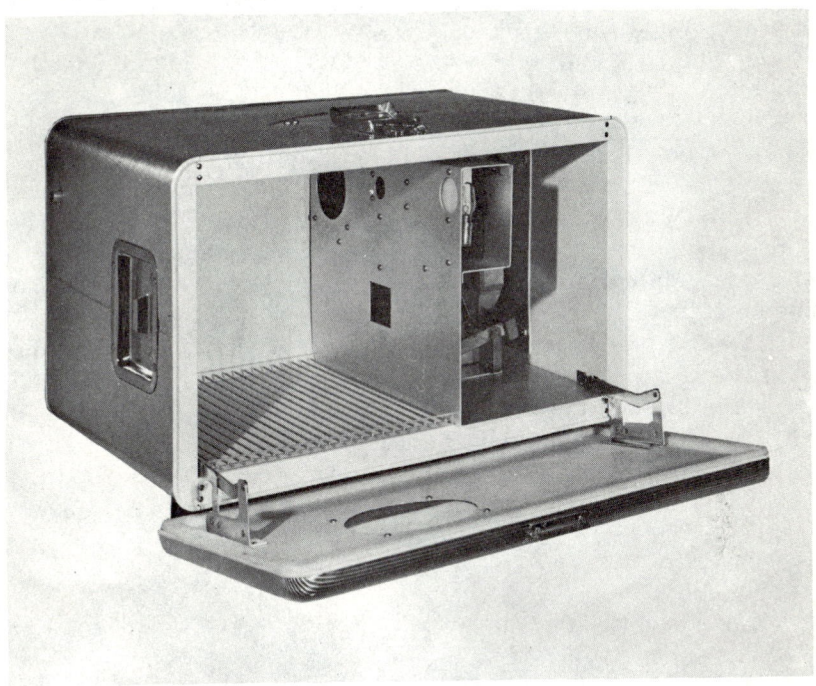

mounted flush to the outside of the thin metal wall. The arm of the lever is accessible to the pigeon through the circular, three-quarter-inch hole in the wall. A force of about fifteen or twenty grams exerted by the pigeon on the arm of the lever operates an electrical switch located near the fulcrum of the lever behind the wall. This signals to the programing and recording equipment that a response has occurred. The closing of the electrical switch defines the operant studied in this apparatus. Usually, the pigeon operates the lever and closes the switch by pecking on the key through the hole in the wall; that is to say, the responses composing this operant are the pigeon's pecks on the key.

The plastic key is translucent. Lights of various colors are arranged behind the wall so as to shine through and illuminate the key. These various colors serve as discriminative stimuli. They are particularly effective because the bird cannot fail to see them as it pecks on the key. Other stimuli may be provided when necessary by varying the intensity or the color of the general illumination, by presenting sounds through the loudspeaker, or by illuminating the key with geometric forms as well as with colors.

The reinforcer is usually about four seconds of access to mixed grain (equal parts of kafir, vetch, and hemp) in a hopper which appears behind the square hole beneath the key. The grain is not accessible except during periods of reinforcement. The reinforcer is presented along with distinctive stimuli: the general illumination and the discriminative stimuli lighting the key are turned off and the grain hopper is lighted brightly from behind the hole. After four seconds of eating, the lighting returns to normal. This arrangement makes the reinforcer a clearly noticeable event, the start and finish of which are clearly defined. For special experiments, the apparatus may be modified to allow for more than one operant or more than one reinforcer.

In an experimental session, a single pigeon is enclosed in the chamber for a period of several hours, usually two or three. During the entire session, the programing apparatus makes the changes in the discriminative stimuli and in the presentations of the reinforcer called for by the passage of time or by occurrences of the response. The details of the program depend on the particular processes being studied in the experiment.

Figure 2.3 A close-up of the experimental chamber used with the rat or small squirrel monkey. *Courtesy of the Grason-Stadler Company, Inc.*

Operant Apparatus for the Rat and Monkey

The operant conditioning apparatus for the rat and monkey is essentially the same as that for the pigeon. Figure 2.3 shows a close-up of the chamber for a rat or a small squirrel monkey. The operant studied in this sort of apparatus is also defined by the activation of a lever. This lever, however, extends out into the chamber. (The chamber in the figure is equipped with two levers.) The lever is usually activated by depression with the paws, although the class of responses composing the operant may include any behavior that operates the lever. Although all kinds of discriminative stimuli may be effectively used with monkeys, those used with the rat differ in intensity and spatial location rather than in color. The reinforcer is usually in the form of pellets of dry food or a liquid (either water or a sweetened liquid diet similar to Metrecal). The apparatus in the figure is designed to dispense pellets into the hole in the lower center of the front wall. If a liquid reinforcer is used, it is made available for short periods of time in an automatic dipper reached through a hole in the floor. Distinctive stimuli accompany either the delivery of the pellets or the periods of access to the liquid reinforcer in the dipper.

PROGRAMING EQUIPMENT

Neither the programing nor the recording equipment varies appreciably with the species of the experimental animal. The programing equipment consists of electrically operated switches, timers, counters, and other devices. They are wired into circuits to determine the sequence of environmental events within the chamber and to bring the events into specified relationships with occurrences of the response.

There are many reasons why automatic electrical equipment is essential in experiments in behavioral research. First, the programs and the alternatives within the experiments are often too complex for a person to handle efficiently, if at all. Also, the two- or three-hour length of the sessions would put severe burdens on a person's efficiency. The automatic equipment easily, reliably, and objectively handles complex decisions throughout the entire experimental session.

Another reason for the use of automatic equipment is the speed required. As we shall see throughout this book, the effect of the environment on behavior depends critically on the timing of envi-

Figure 2.4 The cumulative recorder. *Courtesy of the Ralph Gerbrands Company, Inc.*

ronmental events in relation to behavior. The human reaction time, at its best about one fifth of a second, is simply too long and too variable for the purpose. The automatic equipment operates efficiently and essentially invariably in less than one tenth the time.

Another advantage of automatic equipment is the freedom it affords the researcher. Instead of tediously watching the organism hour after hour, day after day, the researcher is freed by automation for more fruitful use of his time. Freedom from human intervention during the experimental session also means freedom from bias. The experimenter does not have to guess whether or not the lever was pressed each time the rat's paws touch it. The equipment decides, always according to the same criterion.

Not the least advantage of automatic equipment is that it allows for the exact repetition of the experiment in another laboratory next door or halfway around the world. All one experimenter needs to do in order to repeat another's experiment is obtain an exact description of the chamber and the details of the programing and reproduce them faithfully. This possibility of unambiguous replication of experiments has done more than any other single factor to encourage the growth of operant conditioning as a science of behavior.

THE CUMULATIVE RECORDER

The most common recording device in operant conditioning is the *cumulative recorder*. This machine provides a graph of the cumulated (total) number of responses as a function of time. Such a recorder is shown in Figure 2.4 and is schematized in Figure 2.5.

During an experimental session, a motor feeds the paper out at a constant speed. Each operation of the key or lever moves the pen up one step. Thus, time is measured along the length of the paper (the abscissa), while responses are counted across its width (the ordinate). A continuous record of the behavior for the entire session appears in the resulting graph. When the pen reaches the top of the paper, usually after one thousand responses, it resets to the bottom and begins to trace another record beginning with the next response.

Other events within the chamber can also be indicated on the record. The occurrence of the reinforcer is traditionally indicated by a

Figure 2.5 A schematic drawing of the cumulative recorder. The paper unrolls under the two pens as time passes. Each occurrence of the response moves the response-marking pen up one unit toward the top of the paper. Reinforcement is indicated by the hatch-marks on the cumulative record. Additional events during an experimental session can be indicated along the horizontal line at the bottom (or top) of the record by means of the event-marking pen.

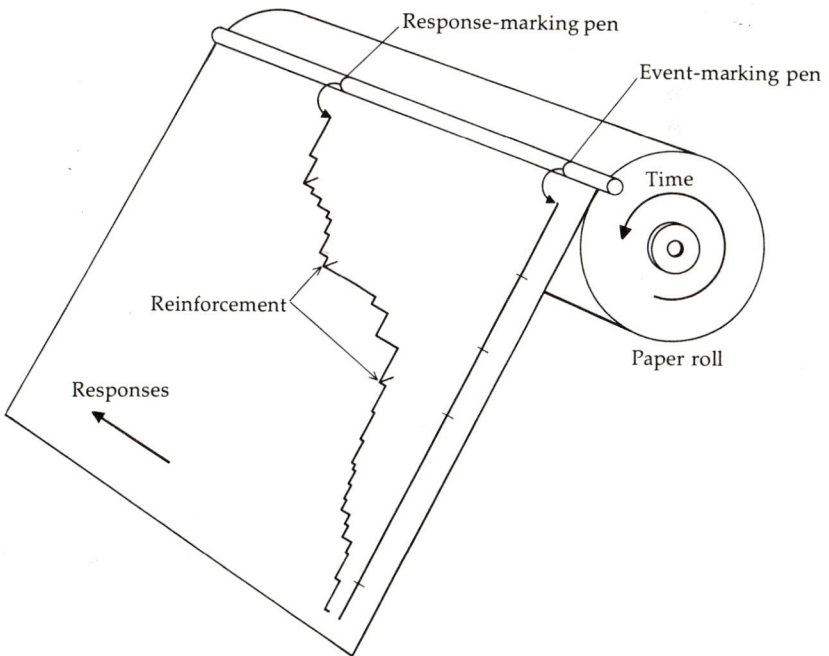

temporary displacement of the pen downward, making a mark on the record. Additional events may be indicated by stationary pens at the top or bottom of the record.

Cumulative records are especially useful in studying the rate of occurrence of the response, because this rate and its changes over time can be easily read from the slope of the cumulative record. Since the paper moves at a constant speed, responding at a high rate produces a steep graph, infrequent responding produces a flat, nearly horizontal graph, and all intermediate rates of responding produce graphs of intermediate slope. Changes in the rate or probability of responding over time, as a function of the experimental manipulations, are reflected in changes in the slope of the record.

The cumulative recorder is supplemented in most experiments by a variety of other recording devices, such as electrical counters which record only the total number of responses in a given period of time and timers which may record the time between responses, between responses and stimuli, or between other successive events.

three

Acquisition and extinction of operant behavior

When we wish to explain the appearance or disappearance of behaviors in an animal's repertoire, we turn first to the principles governing acquisition and extinction. Acquisition in operant conditioning involves either an increase in the frequency with which an operant occurs or the appearance of a previously unobserved operant. Because of the nature of operant behavior, these two kinds of acquisition are not really separate, but they are distinguished for the sake of convenience. Extinction in operant conditioning involves a decrease in the frequency with which an operant occurs when it is no longer reinforced. Before we turn to the methods and procedures for selectively increasing and decreasing the probability of occurrence of existing operant behavior and for creating new operant behavior, we will take a brief look at these questions in the case of respondents.

ACQUISITION OF RESPONDENT BEHAVIOR

Acquisition in the case of respondents is a simple matter, because both the initial occurrence of respondents and their rate of occurrence depend almost completely on the presentation of the eliciting stimuli. There are other variables of importance in most specific instances, but they can, for the present, be considered negligible. Therefore, in order to bring forth a respondent never before performed, it is only necessary to present an effective eliciting stimulus to the organism. In order to enhance selectively the rate at which an organism engages in a particular bit of respondent behavior, it is only necessary to present its eliciting stimulus at a higher rate.

A respondent changes little if at all during the lifetime of the organism. However, as was mentioned in Chapter 1, a new and previously ineffective stimulus may come to elicit the respondent. This phenomenon will be discussed in greater detail in Chapter 8.

ACQUISITION OF OPERANT BEHAVIOR

Operants, on the other hand, have no eliciting stimuli. There is no stimulus, for example, which will elicit the word *operant* from all children or a lever-press from all rats. The creation of new operants and the selective enhancement of the frequency of existing operants are brought about not by any eliciting stimuli which precede the behavior but by the reinforcing stimuli which follow the behavior. Reinforcers, as we have seen in Chapter 1, are simply those stimuli that result in an increase in the frequency of the behavior which they follow.

Increasing the Frequency of Operant Behavior

In order to increase the rate of occurrence of a response already in the animal's repertoire, it is only necessary to follow occurrences of the response with a reinforcing stimulus. For example, if an audience responds in a positive manner—smiling or nodding in agreement—following the occurrence of one particular gesture emitted by a speaker in making a point, the rate at which this gesture occurs will increase. However, before the rate of an operant response can be increased, it is always necessary to wait for an occurrence of the response, because there is no eliciting stimulus which produces it.

Shaping Operant Behavior

Since we must wait for the occurrence of a response before reinforcing it, it may at first seem impossible to create new operant behavior. However, new operant behavior can be created by a process called *shaping*, which uses a combination of reinforcement and nonreinforcement to change existing simple responses into new and more complex responses. In order to understand how shaping is done and how it works, we must first consider some of the effects of reinforcement and nonreinforcement on behavior.

Positive Reinforcement and Activity

Positive reinforcement of a response results not only in a substantial increase in the frequency of that particular response but also in an increase in the frequency of many other bits of the organism's behavior. The extent of the increase in each case depends on a variety of factors, some of which will be discussed in Chapter 4. The frequency of some of the behaviors that are not directly reinforced increases substantially, while the increases in the frequency of other behaviors are so small that they are virtually nonexistent.

The effect of positive reinforcement, then, is to raise the organism's general level of activity. If we reinforce one response of a young child, the child will not only repeat that response but will also emit a flurry of other, varied responses. Positive reinforcement results in an active organism. This property of positive reinforcement plays an important part in shaping. It also makes it extremely difficult to reinforce inactivity.

Positive Reinforcement and Topography

Reinforcement affects not only the frequency but also the topography of responses. *Topography* refers to the physical nature of the responses which compose the operant. Thus, reinforcement modifies the exact form, force, and duration of successive responses, even though each reinforced response counts as an equivalent instance of the operant regardless of its particular form, force, and duration. For example, in the operant of lever pressing, the response that depresses the lever may involve the left or right paw, a forceful or weak depression, or a short or long depression. Whenever one topographical variation is consistently reinforced, either by chance or because of the structure of the organism or the apparatus, that topography comes to predominate. Thus, if the organism happens to emit several short and forceful depressions in succession and each is reinforced, the class of responses composing the operant will come to contain predominantly short and forceful depressions of the lever. Reinforcement, therefore, not only increases the frequency of occurrence of the operant, pressing the lever, but it also changes the topography of the responses involved in pressing the lever.

In the preceding example, short, forceful lever-presses just happened to occur and were reinforced. We may, however, deliberately arrange the experimental apparatus so that only forceful, short presses are reinforced. In this case, we have changed the definition of the operant. Formerly, just about any movement would depress the bar and was thus an instance of the operant. Now, only short, forceful presses will move the bar enough to be considered instances of the operant. Whether selective reinforcement is fortuitous or systematic, the result is the same: short, forceful lever-presses come to predominate. In the first case, we say that the topography of responses has changed, since responses with other topographies will be reinforced if they occur. In the second case, a change has been made in the definition of the operant, because behavior with other topographies will not be reinforced. Although the result is the same, the distinction is important in analyzing the environmental causes of changes in the topography of responses.

Some Effects of Extinction

Extinction refers to a procedure in which an operant that has previously been reinforced is no longer reinforced. The primary effect of extinction is a gradual decrease in the frequency of the operant. However, the behavior does not simply drop out or fade away. In fact, when reinforcement is first discontinued, the frequency of responding may temporarily increase before beginning its decline. Extinction also produces changes in the topography of the responses: at the start of extinction, the form of the behavior becomes more variable and its force increases.

Consider the familiar response of opening a door. This response usually consists of a rotating movement of the hand on the knob followed by a push, and it is usually reinforced by the opening of the door. Now suppose that no matter how many times the door is tried, it does not open. This constitutes extinction because the response is no longer reinforced. Eventually, the frequency with which the subject tries to open the door will decrease, probably to zero, since we rarely try to open doors that are always locked. First, however, the force of the response will increase — perhaps the knob will be turned violently — and the form of the behavior will change — the other hand may be used and the door may even be kicked. Eventually, if the door still fails to open, the frequency of attempts to open it will decrease, along with the force and the variability of the behavior.

The Shaping Procedure

Because they modify the frequency and topography of responses, reinforcement and extinction are the tools used to create or shape new operant behavior. Before beginning to shape behavior, we must make sure that the reinforcer to be used will be effective. This is accomplished by depriving the organism of the reinforcer for some time before shaping begins. Next, we must analyze the exact behavior to be produced: Precisely what sequence of responses is required? Once we have decided on the final behavior, we are in a position to reinforce closer and closer approximations to it.

The general procedure used in shaping begins by raising the deprived organism's general level of activity. This may be done by reinforcing any of its responses; however, in order to shorten the shaping procedure, a response somewhat similar to the desired response is chosen for reinforcement. Reinforcement is then withdrawn, and, as discussed above, the variability and force of the behavior increase. Before the frequency of the behavior decreases, a response closer to the desired behavior is selected for reinforcement from the more forceful and variable behavior initially produced by extinction. This selective reinforcement increases the frequency of the variation that is reinforced. After this behavior has been firmly established and is occurring frequently, reinforcement is again discontinued, variation again increases for a short time, and a response still closer to the desired one is selected from the variation and is reinforced.

This process is called *shaping* because we actually shape a particular response from the available behavior of the organism in much the same way that a sculptor shapes a statue from the clay he has to work with. Thus, we might begin by reinforcing any movement which the organism makes. Then, we may reinforce only walking, then only walking in one direction, and so forth. By continually narrowing our definition of the response required for reinforcement, we increasingly define and shape the organism's behavior.

The Practice of Shaping

Now that we have seen the basic principles and procedures used in shaping, let us use them to shape the behavior of a pigeon so that the bird will press down a pedal protruding an inch or so from the side of its cage at a height of about two inches above the floor. This is a response which the pigeon will very rarely make under ordinary circumstances.

Our first task is to arrange for the immediate reinforcement of responses. Delayed reinforcement is not as effective as immediate reinforcement, partially because it allows the organism to emit additional behavior between the response we wish to reinforce and the actual occurrence of the reinforcer. Thus, the intervening behavior is also reinforced, with the result that what is reinforced is the response followed by some other behavior rather than just the response alone. If we wish to reinforce the response of lifting the hand off the table, for example, it is not efficient to present the reinforcer when the hand is already being replaced on the table. We need a reinforcer that can be presented immediately after the lifting of the hand. Only then is the lifting alone reinforced.

The practical solution to the problem of providing immediate reinforcement is the use of a discriminative stimulus as a conditioned reinforcer. Auditory and visual stimuli can be presented immediately following any response we select, while food, for example, cannot follow the response immediately because the organism must emit additional responses to approach and ingest the food. In order to establish a discriminative stimulus as a conditioned reinforcer, we reinforce a response with food in the presence of a stimulus. For a pigeon, grain is a good reinforcer (provided that the bird has been deprived of grain), and the sound of the grain-delivery mechanism and a decrease of illumination in the bird's chamber have proved to be effective discriminative stimuli. Thus, we reinforce the behavior of walking to the grain and eating only in the presence of the sound of the operation of the grain magazine and decreased illumination. The grain is withdrawn after the pigeon has eaten a few pieces, and it is then presented again and again along with the stimuli. Several presentations of the stimuli and several reinforcements of the response in their presence may be needed to establish the control of the stimuli over the response. When the bird goes immediately and reliably to the grain each time the noise and the decreased illumination occur and does not go there when they do not occur, the discriminative stimuli are in control of the behavior and may be used as a conditioned reinforcer in shaping other behavior.

Notice that this procedure has established a chain of stimuli and responses, as was discussed at the end of Chapter 1. A response during shaping can now be reinforced by the conditioned reinforcer of the noise of the magazine and the decrease in illumination. These stimuli are, in turn, discriminative stimuli, in whose presence the behavior of approaching and taking the grain will be reinforced by the ingestion of the grain.

Primary positive reinforcers, such as the grain, are usually effective only if the organism has been deprived of them in the recent past. (Deprivation as a motivational consideration will be discussed in Chapter 10.) In practice, grain is an extremely effective reinforcer for the pigeon if the pigeon's weight is kept at about eighty per cent of the weight it attains when allowed to feed freely. The value of eighty per cent not only makes grain an effective reinforcer, but it also keeps the bird active and alert.

Now that we have made sure that we have an effective reinforcer for our experiment in shaping, we must analyze the specific behavior to be shaped. In this case, we want the pigeon to walk to the pedal, place a foot on it, and depress it. Now we can begin to shape the pigeon's behavior by reinforcing with the conditioned reinforcer the first part of the response, walking. Or better, if the bird initially walks a great deal, we reinforce the more specific response of walking toward the pedal. Positive reinforcement, the food which the bird obtains in the presence of the conditioned reinforcer, will produce an increase in the bird's general level of activity. After a few presentations of food, the bird will be active, and we will have no difficulty selecting for reinforcement any activity that brings it closer to the pedal. A few reinforcements of walking toward the pedal will result in the bird's walking directly toward the pedal after it has eaten.

The next step is to reinforce the lifting of one foot when the bird is in front of the pedal. Since the bird walks to the pedal, this is not difficult, but it requires careful observation. It is necessary to reinforce immediately the lifting of the leg and not its replacement on the floor. Now, when the bird is in front of the pedal, we selectively reinforce those lifts of the leg which include the leg's movement toward the pedal and are high enough to place the foot above it. This will eventually bring the foot onto the pedal. Finally, we reinforce only depressions of the pedal, and the desired response has been shaped.

The careful and systematic application of the shaping procedure with an effective reinforcer is sufficient to teach any organism any operant behavior of which it is physically capable. For example, pigeons have been shaped to play ping-pong, rats to lift weights well over their own weight, and children to type acceptably at the age of two or three years. The potential of shaping for the behavioral capacity of both animals and men has hardly begun to be explored or exploited.

DEPENDENCIES, CONTINGENCIES, AND SUPERSTITIOUS BEHAVIOR

Sometimes changes in behavior are brought about by deliberate and systematic manipulations of the environment, and sometimes they happen by chance. We noted this difference above in discussing the effects of reinforcement on topography. In the shaping procedure, we have seen how deliberate selective reinforcement changes old behavior into new; now we shall examine a process in which changes in behavior are largely a matter of chance.

Environmental events may have either contingent or dependent relations with behavior. An environmental event is said to be *dependent* on behavior if the event *must*, by the nature of the situation, occur following the behavior. An environmental event is said to be *contingent* on behavior if the event does in fact follow the behavior but *need not* do so. For example, electrical circuitry determines that the lights must go out in a room when the switch is thrown. Thus, the relation between the behavior of turning the switch and the consequential darkness is dependent. The relation between turning the switch and other ensuing events, such as perhaps the bark of a dog in the next house, is likely to be contingent. There is no necessary connection between the thrown switch and the bark, but throwing the switch may occasionally be followed by a bark. Some contingencies are more reliable than others.

The distinction between contingencies and dependencies will prove extremely useful in the analysis of behavior as a whole and particularly in the analysis of the control of behavior by occasional reinforcement. The reader should note, however, that the word *contingency* and the phrase *contingencies of reinforcement* are very frequently used in the current literature to refer to all relationships that are involved in the reinforcement of behavior, whether they be contingencies or dependencies. Nevertheless, as we shall see, the distinction we have made between them is real and important.

Superstitious behavior results from the chance reinforcement of behavior, a true contingency. Suppose that a reinforcer is presented every fifteen seconds, no matter what the organism happens to be doing. Each presentation reinforces the behavior that occurs immediately before it, even though the behavior has nothing to do with the reinforcement. The frequency of the reinforced behavior increases, thus increasing the likelihood that it will be repeated just before the next occurrence of the reinforcer. This process of reinforcement of the behavior that happens to occur is repeated every fifteen seconds, and gradually, quite elaborate sequences of behaviors may be acquired. These sequences are called *superstitions* because they have absolutely nothing to do with the occurrence of the reinforcer. For example, rain dances do not cause rain; but they persist because they are occasionally reinforced by a downpour.

EXTINCTION OF OPERANT BEHAVIOR

We have seen that extinction involves the nonreinforcement of a previously reinforced response, which sooner or later results in reducing the frequency of responding to a very low level. Usually, extinction virtually eliminates responding or brings it back to (or near) its level before reinforcement. We have also seen that extinction does not usually produce an immediate decrease in the frequency of the response. Rather, there is often a brief increase in responding immediately following the onset of extinction. The topography of the response also changes at the start extinction, and the response becomes more forceful and variable for a short time.

The course of extinction varies a great deal, depending on the

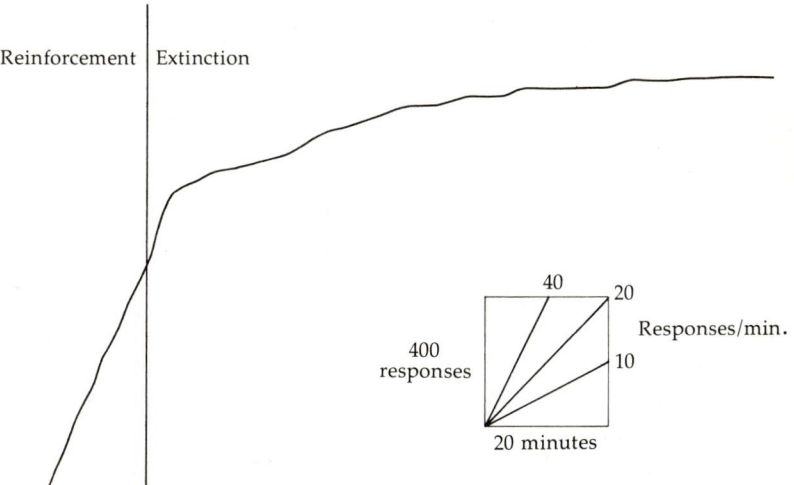

Figure 3.1 A representative cumulative record of responding during extinction after reinforcement.

organism's experiences prior to and during extinction. The progress of extinction is best followed on a cumulative record, such as the one shown in Figure 3.1. The record shows a short, temporary increase in rate followed by a gradual decline which ends in a very low rate of responding (the record runs almost parallel to the abscissa).

The course of extinction can be summarized in terms of three of its parameters: the rate of decline in response frequency, the total number of responses emitted before responding either ceases or reaches some final, low level, and this final level below which the frequency does not sink over a reasonably long time. These parameters of extinction are influenced by a large number of variables, some of which act before extinction begins and some of which act while extinction is in progress. Together, these parameters determine what is called a *resistance to extinction*—a rough estimate of the persistence of the tendency to emit the response after the response is no longer reinforced.

Some Variables Affecting Extinction

The most important variable affecting the course of extinction is the schedule of reinforcement on which the operant was previously maintained. A *schedule of reinforcement* is a rule that tells which occurrences of a particular response will be reinforced. So far, we have dealt only with the extinction of an operant maintained by *continuous reinforcement*—that is, by reinforcement of every occurrence of the operant. However, reinforcement does not have to be continuous to be effective; in fact, *intermittent reinforcement* on a schedule is probably more common than continuous reinforcement. Such a schedule of intermittent reinforcement might, for example, prescribe that only every other occurrence of the response will be reinforced. As we will see in Chapters 6 and 7, there is an almost unlimited number of possible schedules of reinforcement.

Each schedule of reinforcement is followed by a characteristic and predictable pattern of responding during extinction. (These characteristic patterns are treated in Chapters 6 and 7.) The general effect of schedules of intermittent reinforcement is to make responding *more* resistant to extinction. In fact, under some schedules of intermittent reinforcement, resistance to extinction becomes fantastically high.

The magnitude of the reinforcer and the number of reinforcements received prior to extinction also affect the course of extinction. Generally the greater the magnitude of the reinforcer or the number of reinforced responses, the greater the resistance to extinction in terms of both the time and number of responses required to reach a low, terminal rate of responding. The effects of these variables, however, are heavily modulated by the effects of the schedule of reinforcement.

Another variable influencing extinction is the number of previous extinctions experienced by the organism. The larger the number of previous extinctions, the more rapidly will extinction proceed. Organisms whose responses have been reinforced and then extinguished a large number of times generally exhibit very rapid extinction once reinforcement ceases. Apparently, through association with nonreinforcement, the occurrence of a number of unreinforced responses (or of a period of time without reinforced responses) becomes a discriminative stimulus associated with nonreinforcement and, hence, itself occasions a low rate of responding.

The magnitude of the organism's motivation during extinction can also affect the progress of extinction. Extinction is generally slower when it is carried out under more intense deprivation than prevailed during reinforcement. The effects of motivation and of the number of previous extinctions are small, however, when compared to the effects of the schedule of reinforcement.

Spontaneous Recovery

Once the decrease in responding begins, extinction usually proceeds continuously during any one experimental session. At the start of each session, however, the rate of responding is often higher than the rate which prevailed at the end of the previous session. Moreover, the longer the time between successive sessions of extinction, the larger the difference between the rates at the end of one session and at the beginning of the next session. This phenomenon is called *spontaneous recovery* because the rate of responding seems to return spontaneously to a higher level during the time between experimental sessions.

Spontaneous recovery represents responding in the presence of one set of stimuli—those associated with the beginning of the session—in whose presence the responses were previously reinforced. In order for extinction to be complete, it is necessary to extinguish the responses in the presence of each of the discriminative stimuli that have come to control the responses during the previous period of reinforcement. The stimulus conditions prevailing *during* the experimental session compose only one set of these discriminative stimuli. Another set is composed of the stimuli prevailing at the *start* of the session—for example, the recent entry of the animal into the chamber. Spontaneous recovery seems to reflect the control of responding by the latter stimuli.

four

Stimulus control
of operant behavior

Each reinforcement not only increases the probability of reoccurrence of the operant that it follows but also contributes to bringing the operant under the control of the stimuli that are present when
the operant is reinforced. After the responses composing the operant
have been reinforced in the presence of a particular stimulus a number of times, that stimulus comes to control the operant, i.e., the
frequency of those responses is high in the presence of the stimulus
and lower in its absence.

DISCRIMINATIVE STIMULI

In Chapter 1, we said that these controlling stimuli are called
discriminative stimuli. A discriminative stimulus is a stimulus in
whose presence a particular bit of operant behavior is highly probable because the behavior has previously been reinforced in the
presence of that stimulus. We have also said that although discriminative stimuli precede responses, they do not elicit responses. Rather,
discriminative stimuli are said to *occasion* operant responses. A discriminative stimulus *sets the occasion* on which the operant has previously been reinforced.

Because a response under the control of a discriminative stimulus is more frequent in the presence of that stimulus, the frequency
of the response may be controlled by controlling the stimulus: it may
be increased by presenting the stimulus or decreased by withholding

the stimulus. However, the relationship between the controlling stimulus and the response is always probabilistic, since controlling stimuli only increase or decrease the chances that a response will occur. The presentation of the controlling stimulus never guarantees that the response will follow, as does the presentation of an eliciting stimulus. However, under appropriate circumstances, the chances are so high that we can be virtually certain that the response will occur when the discriminative stimulus is presented. In that case, even though the stimulus is in fact discriminative, it may seem to elicit the response.

In the last chapter, we saw that the effect of reinforcement on the probability of reoccurrence of the response is essentially instantaneous. The controlling power of a discriminative stimulus, however, develops gradually: several reinforced responses in the presence of the stimulus are always required before the stimulus effectively controls the response.

STIMULUS GENERALIZATION

Stimulus control is not an entirely selective process. Reinforcement of responses in the presence of one stimulus increases the tendency to respond not only in the presence of that stimulus but also in the presence of other stimuli, though to a lesser degree. When this occurs, an organism is said to *generalize* among stimuli. Generalization is defined functionally: An organism or its behavior is said to generalize to all those stimuli in whose presence the rate of responding increases after the response has been reinforced in the presence of one other stimulus.

Examples of stimulus generalization are plentiful. When a child is reinforced for calling his father "dada," he initially calls other people "dada" as well, though less readily. When a dog is trained to sit at the command "Sit," it initially tends to sit at any forceful, monosyllabic exclamation. When a pigeon's pecks on a red key are reinforced, it initially pecks, though less frequently, on keys of other colors. In each instance, reinforcement of a response in the presence of one stimulus increases the probability of responding not only in the presence of that stimulus but also in the presence of other stimuli.

Directions of Generalization

The stimuli to which generalization occurs can be determined only by empirical methods of experiment and observation. Fortunately, there are some general ground rules that are more or less dependable in predicting the directions generalization will take. One rule is that generalization occurs to stimuli that are composed of the same physical parameters and differ only in the value of the parameters. For example, generalization readily occurs to visual stimuli that differ in color and brightness. Thus, if a pigeon's pecks are reinforced in the presence of a bright red light, the pigeon will be much more likely to exhibit an increased rate of pecking in the presence of a dim green light than in the presence of an auditory stimulus.

Another rule applies to complex stimuli composed of separable parts. Generalization can be expected to occur to stimuli which have perceptible aspects in common with the stimulus that originally set the occasion for reinforcement. For example, if a pigeon's pecks on a triangle have been reinforced, the pigeon will be more likely to peck at stimuli with straight edges or sharp corners than to peck at circles or ovals, because stimuli with edges and sharp corners have those elements in common with the triangle.

Outside of the experimental laboratory, generalization is not often so easily analyzed as these two rules imply. The major difficulty is that it is not always clear simply from observation which stimulus controls the behavior. There is no replacement for experiment when the effective controlling stimulus is in doubt. A stimulus can be identified as being in control of behavior only when it can be demonstrated that the probability or frequency of occurrence of the behavior is different in the presence of the stimulus than in the absence of the stimulus.

When two objects have elements and dimensions in common, we are likely to say that they are similar. However, it is fundamentally incorrect and misleading to believe that the similarity we observe between stimuli is an explanation of generalization. It is not correct to say that an organism generalizes between stimuli *because* they appear similar to us and presumably to it. Rather, our labeling of stimuli as "similar" is a demonstration of our own tendency to generalize between or among them: it shows that we have responded to them in somewhat the same manner. We simply share this tendency with the organism whose behavior we observe.

Stimulus Generalization vs. Frequent, Uncontrolled Responding

Stimulus generalization must be distinguished from a simple increase in the overall tendency to emit the reinforced response regardless of the stimulus. Generalization is an increase in the frequency of responding which is *dependent on the stimulus*. Therefore, in order to attribute the occurrence of a response in the presence of a stimulus to generalization, we must show that the increased frequency does not occur in the absence of the stimulus. For example, in order to attribute a child's calling another person "dada" to generalization from the reinforcement of the response "dada" in the presence of the father, we must be sure that the emission of the response depends on the appearance of another person and that it does not simply reflect the fact that reinforcement has caused the child to repeat the word frequently.

Response Generalization

Reinforcement of an operant results not only in an increase in the frequency of the responses composing that operant but also in an increase in the frequency of similar responses. Thus, after reinforcement of the response "dada," a child will be more likely to say "baba" and "gaga," as well as "dada." This phenomenon is called *response generalization.* Continued reinforcement of "dada" and lack of reinforcement of other responses results in a preponderance of "dada" in the child's vocabulary. As we have seen in Chapter 3, this process is fundamental in the shaping of behavior.

Measurement of Stimulus Generalization

The amount of stimulus generalization is expressed by the relationship between the rates of responding prevailing in the presence of each of a group of stimuli before and after reinforcement in the presence of one of them. For example, the following experiment describes the measurement of a pigeon's generalization to stimuli of different colors. The response to be measured is the pigeon's pecking on a key, and the discriminative stimuli are the illumination of the experimental chamber by red, orange, yellow, green, and blue lights.

First, before we reinforce any of the pigeon's responses, we measure the rate of responding in the presence of each stimulus by presenting the stimuli to the pigeon individually and counting the responses made in the presence of each. Responding before reinforcement is infrequent, as is shown by the typical rates in Figure 4.1 (the circles). The number of pecks per minute in the presence of each color ranges from zero to five.

Since these rates of responding are typically very low, it has become customary to dispense with this part of the measurement of generalization. Its purpose is to be sure that there is no pronounced tendency to respond to one stimulus more than to another at the beginning of the experiment, since such a tendency could confound

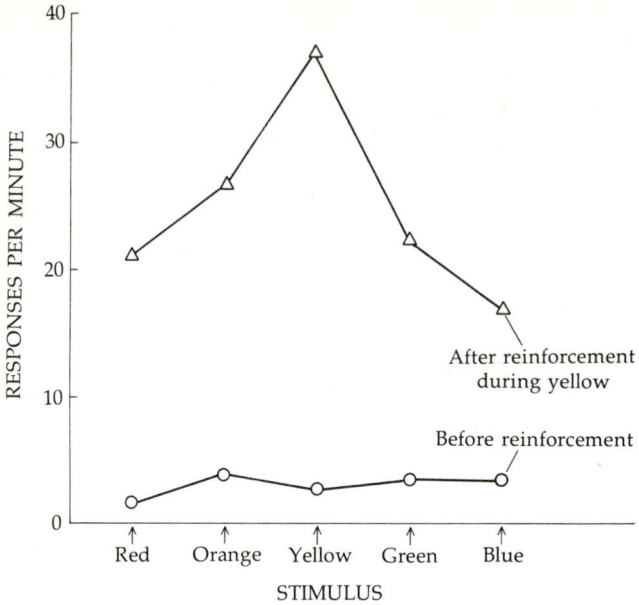

Figure 4.1 A gradient of generalization to the color of a light.

the results of the measurements. It is wise, therefore, to make these initial measurements, but traditional not to bother.

The next step in the measurement of generalization is reinforcement of the response, pecking, in the presence of one stimulus only—in this case, yellow illumination—for several hour-long daily sessions. Then, reinforcement is discontinued, and during extinction, the number of responses in the presence of each stimulus is measured.* In order to make the measurements more reliable, the rate is measured several times in the presence of each stimulus. While the rate of responding is gradually declining because of extinction, each color is presented for about thirty seconds until all five colors have been presented. Then they are presented several more times, each time in a different order and with no color being repeated until all the other colors have been presented. Usually five or six presentations of each color are sufficient to ensure reliable measurements.

The triangles on the graph in Figure 4.1 represent the total rate of responding computed for all the presentations of each color. The differences in the rates of responding to the five stimuli are reliable since we can expect that any differences in the rates caused by the

---

*Responding in this experiment is reinforced on a schedule of intermittent reinforcement known as the *variable-interval*. We will be discussing this schedule in Chapter 6. It is used in this experiment because the extinction performance which follows its termination is very smooth and orderly.

progressive decline of responding in extinction have been averaged out by the different orders of presentation of the stimuli. However, because the measurements were made during extinction while the rates were continuously decreasing, the rates cannot be taken to mean anything except the *relative* degree of control which the various colors exert over responding. They have no significance as absolute rates of responding; and it is not meaningful to compare various organisms with respect to these rates because their responding during extinction may decline at different speeds. Birds may, of course, be compared with respect to the *relative* difference between the rates prevailing in two colors, since organisms may differ in the breadth of their generalization. This difference can be measured by comparing the slopes of the curves in graphs like the one shown in Figure 4.1.

As Figure 4.1 illustrates, the effect of generalization is to increase the tendency to respond in the presence of each of the stimuli. The amount by which the rate prevailing before reinforcement in the presence of each stimulus has increased after reinforcement expresses the amount of generalization from the yellow illumination to the other stimuli. All the stimuli now control more responding because of the previous reinforcement of responding in the presence of yellow.

Notice that the amount of generalization becomes less and less the larger the difference between the yellow stimulus and the stimulus in question (as measured by the wavelength of each stimulus). This orderly decrease in responding as the value of the physical property being varied moves farther away from the value in whose presence responding was reinforced is called the *gradient of generalization.*

DISCRIMINATION AND GENERALIZATION

An organism is said to *discriminate* between two stimuli when it behaves differently in the presence of each. If an organism responds identically in the presence of each of two or more stimuli, it does not discriminate between them.

The generalization gradient reveals discrimination, therefore, insofar as the organism responds at a different rate in the presence of each stimulus. The discrimination is by no means perfect: the pigeon does not respond only in the presence of one stimulus and not at all in the presence of another. Rather, the tendency to respond is different in the presence of each. Sometimes the difference is large, as between the rates prevailing with red light and with yellow light in the above experiment. Sometimes it is very small or negligible, as it would be between the rates prevailing in the presence of two yellow lights of only slightly different brightnesses. The difference between the tendencies to respond in the presence of two stimuli is a measure of the degree of the organism's discrimination between the two stimuli.

The Formation of a Discrimination

The discrimination between two stimuli becomes more and more pronounced if differential reinforcement is instituted. When responding is reinforced in the presence of one stimulus and not reinforced in the presence of another stimulus, the difference between the rates of responding in the presence of each of the two stimuli increases; the rate of reinforced responding in the presence of one stimulus remains high or increases, and the rate of unreinforced responding in the presence of the other stimulus decreases. This process is called the *formation of a discrimination*. The result of continued differential reinforcement is to build up a high probability of responding in the presence of one stimulus and a very low probability of responding in the presence of the other stimulus.

It may seem strange to call this process the *formation* of a discrimination when there is usually some difference between responding in the presence of the two stimuli from the beginning. Nevertheless, the term is current, and it covers those few cases in which there is no difference at all between the behaviors in the presence of each of the two stimuli before the beginning of differential reinforcement.

The formation of a discrimination is studied over time. The results of a typical study appear in Figure 4.2. Here the pigeon's pecking is reinforced in the presence of a red key and not reinforced in the presence of a green key. The graph shows the rate of responding in the presence of each stimulus as a function of successive sessions of differential reinforcement. Notice that the difference between the rates prevailing in the presence of the two stimuli is small at first and gradually becomes greater as the number of presentations of the stimuli increases. The small initial difference is due to substantial generalization between the two stimuli. The difference becomes greater as the rate of unreinforced responding declines and the rate of reinforced responding increases.

The Influence of Generalization on the Formation of a Discrimination

The extent of the generalization between two stimuli influences the formation of a discrimination between them in several ways. In

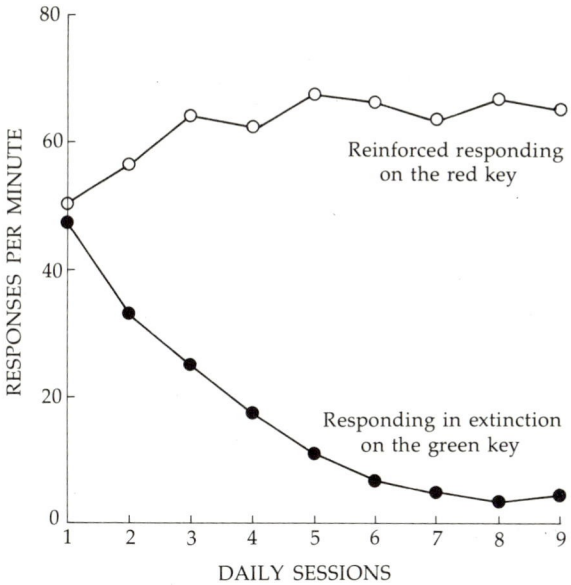

Figure 4.2 The formation of a discrimination.

order to understand these, it is best to review a rather long but basically simple experiment. Suppose that we can make a pigeon's key any one of three colors — red, orange, or yellow — and that these colors are presented in succession a number of times during each daily session. At first (Part 1), for a week of daily sessions, we reinforce responding in the presence of all three stimuli. Then (Part 2), for another week of sessions, we reinforce responding only when the key is red and never when the key is either orange or yellow. Next (Part 3), for a week, we extinguish responding in the presence of all three colors. Finally (Part 4), we again reinforce responding only when the key is red.

The results of this experiment appear in Figure 4.3 in the form of a graph showing the rate of responding in the presence of each of the three stimuli during each session under each of the four procedures described above. These results reveal four effects of generalization on the process of formation of a discrimination:

1. When responding is reinforced only in the presence of the red key, the responding decreases more rapidly in the presence of the yellow key than in the presence of the orange key, even though responding is extinguished in the presence of each. Provided that responding continues to be reinforced in the presence of one stimulus, generalization from that stimulus helps determine how rapidly

responding declines when extinguished in the presence of different stimuli. Thus, the greater generalization from red to orange than from red to yellow slows the decline of responding in the presence of the orange key.

2. As long as responses are reinforced in the presence of the red key, extinction does not reduce the rate of responding in the presence of the other two stimuli to zero. Even after extinction has been continued for some time, there is always some residual responding in the presence of the orange and yellow keys, although reliably less responding in the presence of the yellow key. This unreinforced responding is a result of generalization from the reinforced responding in the presence of red. Thus, as the graph shows, when responding in the presence of red is also extinguished, there is a further decrease in the rate of responding in the presence of both the orange and yellow keys.

3. Extinction produces the most rapid decrease in the rate of responding in the presence of the red key. Because there is no reinforcement in the presence of any other stimulus, extinction is not retarded by generalization from any other stimuli to red.

4. When responding is once again reinforced in the presence of the red key only, the rates of responding to orange and yellow eventually return to the former low level that prevailed in Part 2 of the

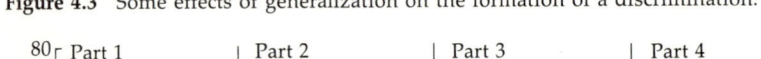

Figure 4.3 Some effects of generalization on the formation of a discrimination.

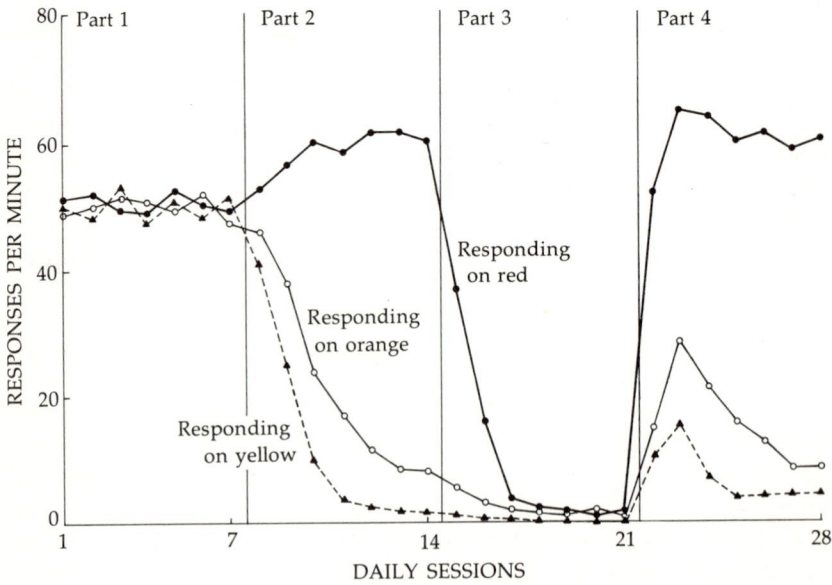

experiment, when the procedure was identical. This result is preceded, however, by a surge of responding up to a medium rate in the presence of orange and yellow and to a reliably higher rate in orange. This rate never exceeds about one half the rate prevailing in red, however; and it gradually decreases to the level maintained by generalization in Part 2.

These four effects of generalization involve changes in the rate of responding in the presence of each of two stimuli which are caused by changes in the consequences (reinforcement or nonreinforcement) of responding in the presence of a different stimulus. The rate of responding in the presence of the yellow key, for example, depends not only on the conditions prevailing during yellow but also on the conditions prevailing during red. Such effects are of fundamental importance in pointing out that the causes of behavior that occurs under a given set of circumstances may include events that occur under different circumstances. More examples of such multiple determination of behavior will come up during our discussion of schedules of reinforcement in Chapters 6 and 7.

Behavioral Contrast and Discrimination

In Parts 1 and 2 of the experiment whose results are shown in Figure 4.3, the conditions of reinforcement were always the same in the presence of the red key. The rate of responding during red was not constant, however. Rather, it increased when responding was no longer reinforced during orange and yellow. This phenomenon accompanies the formation of a discrimination and is called *behavioral contrast*, to differentiate it from generalization. In generalization, the rates of responding in the presence of two stimuli both change in the same direction. In behavioral contrast, the rates in the presence of two stimuli change in opposite directions: in our experiment, the rate decreased in orange and yellow and increased in red. We have an example of generalization when a child's unruly behavior extinguishes more slowly than usual at home because it is reinforced on the playground; we have an example of behavioral contrast when the extinction of unruly behavior at home makes for increasingly frequent unruly behavior on the playground.

Contrast seems to depend on the relation between the reinforcing conditions associated with the two stimuli. When the consequences of a response become less reinforcing in the presence of one stimulus, we can expect the frequency of the response to increase in the presence of another stimulus where its consequences remain reinforcing. Contrast, like generalization, furnishes an example of changes in behavior under one set of circumstances which are caused by changes in the consequences of the behavior under a different set of circumstances.

ATTENTION AND STIMULUS CONTROL

It often happens that reinforcement of a response in the presence of a stimulus does not bring all properties of that stimulus into control over the behavior. Variation or elimination of the noncontrolling property has no effect on the behavior; and if the properties are separated, the generalization gradient across values of that property is flat and unchanging. When this happens, the organism is said to be not *attending* to that property of the stimulus.

As a simple example, the pecking of a pigeon was reinforced in the presence of a white triangle on a red background and was never reinforced in the presence of a white circle on a green background. Subsequently, with no reinforcement, the four parts of these two stimuli were presented separately: the circle and the triangle on grey backgrounds and the colored backgrounds without superimposed figures. None of the birds pecked at either part—circle or the green—of the stimulus in whose presence responding had not been reinforced. Some pecked only at the triangle, some only at the red background, and some at both at various rates. The birds that pecked at the triangle and not at the red background were attending only to the triangle, not to the red; their behavior had been brought under the control of the property of form but not of the property of color of the stimulus that had set the occasion for reinforcement. The behavior was, in all cases, under the control of the original stimulus when both parts were combined, but it was not always under the control of each individual part.

Attention is often directed to one sensory modality to the exclusion of others. For example, suppose that a pigeon's peck is reinforced in the presence of a brightly lighted key and a loud clicking sound from a loudspeaker. The pecking will be likely to come under the control of the brightness of the key and not under the control of the noise. Decreases in the brightness of the key will result in a decreased tendency to respond, while changes in the loudness of the noise will probably have very little or no effect on behavior. A pigeon is more likely to attend to a visual stimulus prominently displayed on the key that it pecks than to a relatively unlocalized noise. Also, pigeons in general have a greater tendency to attend to visual stimuli than to other kinds of sensory stimuli.

There are two factors that help determine which stimulus an organism will attend to at any particular time: the inherited characteristics of the organism and its experiences with its environment.

Inherited Determinants of Attention

Organisms are born with dispositions to attend to particular aspects of the environment. From all the stimuli available in its environment among which it is able to discriminate, the organism selectively attends only to some.

A common example of this phenomenon is the selective control of the cat's behavior by movement, almost to the total exclusion of color and brightness. If a cat is taught to discriminate between a moving, dim, red object and a stationary, bright, green object, the chances are excellent that movement will be the controlling property. The cat will come to respond to moving objects regardless of changes in brightness or hue. This does not mean, of course, that the cat is unable to discriminate brightness: it can easily be conditioned to enter the brighter of two identical chambers if its food is always placed there. Apparently, the cat can even discriminate between colors if color is the only difference between stimuli which are differentially associated with an adequate reinforcer. If left to its own devices, however, the cat is more likely to rely on movement as a stimulus.

Some Environmental Determinants of Attention

The previous experience of an organism may also cause it to attend to one of several stimuli or properties of stimuli, even though all have the same consistent association with the reinforcement of responses. One rule seems to be that once attention to one property has been established, the organism will continue to attend to that property to the relative exclusion of other properties. For example, if the organism has previously made a series of discriminations between stimuli on the basis of brightness, it generally attends to the brightness of the stimuli in future discriminations. If the cat, for example, were placed in a world where movement had no consistent connection with reinforcement but brightness did, then the cat would come to attend selectively to the brightness of stimuli, probably to the exclusion of attention to movement.

It follows from the above rule that once a discrimination has been established on the basis of a relatively large difference in one property of stimuli, the introduction of a smaller difference in another property of stimuli will usually be ignored, unless the conditions of reinforcement are changed. For example, if an organism develops a discrimination between a bright and a dim light and then a slight difference between two faint sounds is added to the discrimination, the organism will rarely attend to the sounds. When the sounds are presented later without the lights, they will have no differential effects on behavior. The lights as stimuli overshadow the sounds.

Supraordinate Stimuli

Supraordinate stimuli inform the organism about the currently relevant property of a group of stimuli. Technically speaking, they are stimuli in whose presence one property rather than another has, in the past, set the occasion for reinforcement of a response. With people, words are the most common supraordinate stimuli. "Tell me the colors of these cards" occasions from the listener responses to the colors rather than the shapes or sizes of the cards. In fact, after hearing these words, the shapes and sizes will control behavior so little that the subject probably will not even be able to recall them later.

Supraordinate stimuli also control the responses of animals. Suppose that a pigeon is exposed sequentially to all four combinations of white figures on colored backgrounds with a triangle and circle as figures and red and green as backgrounds. When the bird's chamber is lighted yellow by a lamp on the side, responding is reinforced in the presence of those two of the four stimuli that contain red; when it is lighted blue, responding is reinforced in the presence of those two of the four stimuli that contain a triangle. The yellow and blue general illuminations indicate whether responses to the ground or to the figure will be reinforced. The bird quickly comes to respond appropriately.

Transferring Stimulus Control

Attention may be transferred from one group of stimuli to another by a procedure of simultaneous presentation of both stimuli followed by the fading of the originally controlling stimulus. Suppose that key pecking is currently under the control of the color of the key (the bird pecks at green and does not peck at red) and that we wish to shift control to geometric figures (so that the bird pecks at a triangle and does not peck at a circle). This could be accomplished by alternately presenting the triangle and the circle, each against a grey background, and by reinforcing pecking on the triangle while extinguishing pecking on the circle. It is more efficient, however, to present the figures initially on the appropriate colored backgrounds (the triangle on green and the circle on red) and then gradually to fade the backgrounds by lessening their intensities. At first the colors control the key pecking; but as the colors become dimmer, the forms come into control. If the fading is carried out at the proper rate, no change in the rate of responding in the presence of either stimulus will occur. Unfortunately, there is no information available on precisely when the new stimuli, the figures, come into control over the behavior. Nor is it known if the shift in attention is gradual or abrupt. But the fact that continued reinforcement in the presence of the triangle and the fading green ground seems to be necessary suggests that the transfer of control is gradual.

Sensory Preconditioning

There is some evidence that transfer of control may sometimes occur without explicit reinforcement. This phenomenon is called *sensory preconditioning*. Two stimuli — for example, a light and a sound — are first presented simultaneously to an organism several times. Then, some response is reinforced in the presence of only one of the stimuli until that stimulus comes to be an effective discriminative stimulus for that response. If the organism is then placed in the presence of only the other stimulus, it is found that the response has come under the control of this second stimulus also. In order to assure that this result is not simply a result of a generalization between the two stimuli, other organisms are trained and tested in the same way, but without the initial exposure to the two stimuli simultaneously. The evidence, which is too intricate to be elaborated here, indicates that sensory preconditioning is effective in transferring control but that the control by the second stimulus is by no means as strong as the control generated by traditional methods. Sensory preconditioning is, of course, effective in producing the first few responses in the presence of the new stimulus, a situation which may be used as the basis for more conclusive procedures.

THE LIMITS OF STIMULUS CONTROL

Although the least discriminable difference between stimuli may be very small, there is a limit to how fine a discrimination can be made. For example, there is a difference between the intensities of two sounds or the brightnesses of two lights that no organism can reliably discriminate, even under the most favorable circumstances. These limits have been extensively studied in the science of psychophysics and have been reliably established for many stimuli and animals.

It is dangerous, however, to maintain that a given organism cannot discriminate between two stimuli without exhaustive attempts to produce the discrimination; only one demonstration of a successful discrimination is needed to disprove the assertion of its impossibility. It is safe to say that all organisms have discriminative capacities that are never fully developed because their environments never provide differential consequences of selective behavior in the presence of minimally different stimuli. The cultured palate of the wine taster, the discerning nostrils of the perfumer, the critical ear of the conductor, the sensitive fingers of the safecracker, and the educated eyes of the painter are familiar illustrations of discriminative capacities that remain relatively untapped in most human beings.

five

Conditioned reinforcers

Some stimuli come to be reinforcers for an organism because of their association with reinforcement in the previous experience of the organism. These stimuli are called *secondary*, or *conditioned*, *reinforcers* in order to distinguish them from *innate, primary,* or *unconditioned reinforcers*, which require no experience to be effective. If it were not for the phenomenon of conditioned reinforcement, we would all be limited to reinforcers whose effectiveness is innate. Instead, through experience, new stimuli are added to the class of effective reinforcers. A fraternity pin, meaningless at an earlier age, reinforces the behavior of a teen-ager. The voice of a dog's master, ineffectual at first, comes to reinforce the dog's behavior. Stock market quotations, at first dull lists of numbers, come to reinforce an investor's behavior. Under special circumstances, conditioned reinforcers may be highly individualized, as in the case of idiosyncratic fetishes.

POSITIVE AND NEGATIVE CONDITIONED REINFORCERS

Just as there are two kinds of primary or innate reinforcers, so there are two kinds of conditioned reinforcers. One kind is composed of stimuli whose appearance or presentation is reinforcing. These are called *positive conditioned reinforcers*. The other is composed of stimuli whose disappearance or withdrawal is reinforcing. These are called *conditioned aversive stimuli* (or, by some, *negative conditioned reinforcers*). Both positive conditioned reinforcers and conditioned aversive stimuli have several effects on behavior, but we are concerned here only with their effects as reinforcers.

FORMATION OF CONDITIONED REINFORCERS

Provided that a stimulus is discriminable and commands attention, it can become a conditioned positive reinforcer or a conditioned aversive stimulus. At the start, we have a stimulus whose presentation or withdrawal following an operant has no effect on the probability of reoccurrence of the responses. After the organism undergoes experience with the stimulus, however, it becomes a reinforcer. The necessary experience turns out to be reinforcement itself. A stimulus in whose presence a positive reinforcer occurs becomes a positive conditioned reinforcer. The conditioned reinforcer is said to be *based on* the reinforcer experienced by the organism in its presence. One interpretation of this process, as we shall see, is that conditioned reinforcers owe their effectiveness to the fact that they function as discriminative stimuli for later responses which are maintained by reinforcement in their presence. A stimulus in whose presence an aversive stimulus occurs becomes a conditioned aversive stimulus. The conditioned aversive stimulus is *based on* the aversive stimulus.

The formation of a conditioned reinforcer is usually a gradual process: several reinforcements or several occurrences of an aversive stimulus are necessary. Eventually, the stimulus takes on the reinforcing or aversive properties of the stimulus presented to the organism in its presence.

It makes little difference whether the reinforcer on which the conditioned reinforcer is based is itself innate or conditioned. A new conditioned positive reinforcer can usually be formed on the basis of either an innate or conditioned positive reinforcer; and a new conditioned aversive stimulus can usually be formed on the basis of either an innate or conditioned aversive stimulus.

As an example of the formation of a conditioned positive reinforcer, suppose that a hungry pigeon's pecking is reinforced with food in the presence of a red light behind its key. During alternating periods when the key is lit by a green light, pecking is not reinforced with food. Rather, pecks on the green key produce the red key. Under these conditions, the pigeon will peck both the red and the green key. It will peck the red key, of course, because pecking the red key is reinforced with food. It will peck the green key because pecking the green key also is reinforced — with a conditioned reinforcer, the red key. The red key has become a conditioned reinforcer because pecks on it have produced food in its presence. The red key can be further demonstrated as a reinforcer by showing that its presentation will reinforce not only pecking on the green key but any response that it follows.

An example of the formation of a conditioned aversive stimulus occurs when an electric shock is delivered to the feet of a rat during periods of noise through a loudspeaker. The noise will become a conditioned aversive stimulus; its termination will reinforce the response which terminates it, just as the termination of the electric shock reinforces responses that terminate the shock.

CHAINS OF RESPONSES AND STIMULI

Conditioned reinforcers generally occur within chains of responses and stimuli. A *chain* is composed of a series of responses joined together by stimuli that act both as conditioned reinforcers and as discriminative stimuli. A chain begins with the presentation of a discriminative stimulus. When the organism makes the appropriate response in the presence of this stimulus, a conditioned reinforcer is presented. This conditioned reinforcer is also a discriminative stimulus which occasions the next appropriate response. This response is reinforced with another conditioned reinforcer, which is also a discriminative stimulus for the next response, and so on. The last stimulus in the chain, on at least some occasions, is a primary, or innate, reinforcer.

One example of a chain of behavior is the sequence of responses we emit when we go out to eat at a restaurant. The initial discriminative stimuli may be a friend's telephone call, the time of day, or a strong hunger contraction. The chain that follows is composed of many responses: rising; opening the door; leaving the house; getting into, starting, driving, and parking the car; entering the restaurant; sitting down; reading the menu; ordering; and eating. The environmental stimulus that follows each response — the open doors, the running engine, the restaurant facade, the appearance of the waiter, the food — occasions the next response in the chain. We do not try to get into our car until the door is open. Nor do we attempt to order food unless there is a waiter at our table. Each of these discriminative stimuli is, in addition, a conditioned reinforcer. The opening of a door, for example, is reinforcing because the open door is a stimulus in whose presence a response is reinforced. The entire chain of behavior is maintained by the food we finally ingest; we simply do not go to restaurants which furnish either bad food or no food at all.

An experimental example of a chain may begin when a pigeon is presented with a blue key. When the pigeon pecks the key, it changes to red. After the key turns red, the pigeon presses a pedal which turns the key yellow. During yellow, displacing a bar changes the key to green. Finally, during green, pecks are reinforced with the operation of a grain-delivery mechanism and its associated stimuli, in the presence of which the bird approaches the grain magazine and eats. Each change of color is a conditioned reinforcer for the response that precedes and produces it as well as a discriminative stimulus for the response emitted in its presence. The entire sequence is maintained by the grain which the pigeon ultimately eats.

The Links in a Chain

Each unit composed of a discriminative stimulus, response, and reinforcer is called a *link* of the chain. The experimental chain described above, for example, has five links: blue – peck – red; red – treadle – yellow; yellow – bar – green; green – peck – grain-magazine operation (and other stimuli); grain magazine – eat – food ingestion. Because each stimulus has a dual function, as discriminative stimulus and conditioned reinforcer, the links overlap. In fact, it is this dual function of the stimuli that holds the chain together.

Theoretically, chains may have any number of links, although in practice there is an upper limit. With some long chains, responding will not occur in the presence of the first stimulus but will begin if the second stimulus is presented instead. In most experimental studies of the basic principles governing chains, three links are used: responding during one stimulus produces another, during which responding produces the primary reinforcer and its associated stimuli, in whose presence the organism moves to consume the reinforcer. The effectiveness of the second stimulus as a conditioned reinforcer is assessed by measuring the behavior which it reinforces in the presence of the first stimulus.

A chain of at least two links is always involved whenever any behavior is emitted in obtaining a primary reinforcer. For example, a rat presses a lever which produces a buzz and the presentation of a liquid diet. On hearing the buzz, the rat moves to eat the reinforcer.

Chains Within Responses

The responses involved in the final link of a chain are usually treated as a single operant, defined in terms of their common effect in the consumption of the reinforcer. However, this operant itself involves a chain, which may also be analyzed into its components. For example, in the presence of the buzz, the rat moves to the food dispenser; once there, it places its head near the hole; with the hole and head properly aligned, the rat licks and swallows. Each response in the chain is reinforced by its consequences.

Such breakdowns as this are often useful or necessary in the refinement of the sequence or the individual topographies of behaviors composing the original, grosser response. For example, if the rat were taking an unnecessarily circuitous route to the food, we could speed it up by selectively changing the consequences of only that bit of behavior in the chain. We could arrange that the move to the magazine will be reinforced only if it is direct.

The fineness to which the analysis of behavior is carried is determined by the purpose of the analysis. Consider the game of golf, for example. If we want to do no more than understand or manipulate the golfer's general proficiency at the game, we need know only the total number of strokes he takes per outing or per week. Each stroke is an instance of a response, without regard for the kind of club he used. If, however, we want to manipulate, and presumably improve, his game, we will have to analyze the play of each individual hole into a chain, probably defining the links of the chain in terms of the club that is employed. This will allow independent manipulations of each stroke since its consequences can be dealt with individually. If, finally, we want to improve the topography of an individual stroke, such as the drive or putt, we must analyze that single set of behaviors into a chain. Then, using such consequences as distance, accuracy, and our approval as the terminal reinforcers in the chain, we attempt to manipulate directly the sequence and topography of the individual movements in the stroke.

Conditioned Reinforcers and Discriminative Stimuli

In chains of stimuli and responses, each stimulus except the first and the last functions as both a conditioned reinforcer and a discriminative stimulus. The two functions are clearly and functionally separate. As a conditioned reinforcer, the stimulus reinforces responses made in the previous link of the chain, those responses which resulted in its appearance. As a discriminative stimulus, the stimulus occasions the behavior emitted in its presence. This behavior is reinforced by the appearance of the stimulus in the next link of the chain, functioning as a conditioned reinforcer.

It is often asked whether these two functions of the stimuli in a chain are always available together for the same stimuli. Can all discriminative stimuli also function as conditioned reinforcers? Can all conditioned reinforcers always function as discriminative stimuli? In theory, the answer to both questions seems to be no; but in practice, the exceptions in each instance are of comparatively negligible importance. For most practical purposes, the functions as conditioned reinforcer and as discriminative stimulus coexist as properties of the same stimulus in a chain.

Consider the first question. All discriminative stimuli cannot also be conditioned reinforcers, because there is a limit to the number of links that will hang together in a chain. Experiments have shown that the farther a stimulus is from the termination of the chain, the less effective it is both as a discriminative stimulus and as a conditioned reinforcer. As the length of the chain is increased (up beyond a dozen or so links with pigeons), there comes a point where the stimulus of the second link is such a weak conditioned reinforcer because of its distance from the final reinforcement of the sequence that it will not reinforce the response in the first link. However, this stimulus of the second link is still effective as a discriminative stimulus; it will occasion at least the one response necessary for advancement into the third link. This of course means that the stimulus of the third link is an effective conditioned reinforcer. The fact remains, however, that the stimulus of the second link will cease to function as a conditioned reinforcer even though it continues to function as a discriminative stimulus. Because of the limit on the number of links in a chain, this state of affairs must be reached eventually if the number of links is continually increased. Except for this limit, discriminative stimuli can be counted on to be effective conditioned reinforcers.

The second question is whether a conditioned reinforcer, having been present when a particular bit of behavior was reinforced, will necessarily function as a discriminative stimulus for that behavior. This necessarily happens in chains, where a particular response is reinforced in each link by the presentation of the stimulus that functions as the discriminative stimulus of the next link. It also occurs if we set up a series of stimuli which will occur in sequence regardless of the response emitted by the organism. If any of the stimuli we present are conditioned reinforcers, they will reinforce whatever behavior happens to precede them. Thus, as we saw in Chapter 3, the usual result is a chain of regular, although not required and therefore superstitious, behavior. Since each conditioned reinforcer has accompanied the reinforcer on which it is based, the conditioned reinforcer will fail to function as a discriminative stimulus only if neither a particular, required response nor regular, superstitious behavior has been conditioned by the other reinforcer. Although this state of affairs is conceivable, it probably never actually occurs.

THE STRENGTH OF CONDITIONED REINFORCERS

The strength of a conditioned reinforcer is measured in terms of its durability and its potency. *Durability* refers to the length of time or number of responses a conditioned reinforcer will continue to reinforce if the reinforcer on which it is based is discontinued. The *potency* of a conditioned reinforcer is measured in terms of the rate of responding which it is able to maintain.

Durability

A conditioned reinforcer gradually becomes ineffective if responding in its presence is no longer followed, at least occasionally, by the reinforcer on which it is based. The longer the conditioned reinforcer remains effective after the other reinforcer has been discontinued, the more durable it is said to be. The reinforcer on which the conditioned reinforcer is based may be either a primary reinforcer or a conditioned reinforcer whose effectiveness is itself maintained at least once in a while by a primary reinforcer, either in its presence or at the end of a chain to which the conditioned reinforcer belongs. At the same time, as the reinforcing effectiveness of a conditioned reinforcer decreases—as it does in extinction—the tendency to respond in the presence of the conditioned reinforcer decreases also. The decreases in the effectiveness of the stimulus as a conditioned reinforcer and as a discriminative stimulus usually proceed at roughly the same speed. This means that all of the factors that prolong the course of extinction in the presence of a stimulus also prolong the period of time and the number of presentations during which the stimulus will be an effective conditioned reinforcer.

Potency

Different conditioned reinforcers used in exactly the same way may differ in their effectiveness as reinforcers: one reinforcer may maintain a higher rate of responding than another. The higher the rate of responding maintained by presentations of the conditioned reinforcer, the higher the potency of that reinforcer.

The potency of a conditioned reinforcer—that is, its ability to maintain a rate of responding—is determined by many factors. The following are four of the most important factors.

1. The potency of a conditioned reinforcer increases with higher frequencies of presentation in its presence of the primary or conditioned reinforcer on which it is based. The evidence suggests that this function is concave downward; that is to say, as the frequency of presentation becomes higher and higher, the potency of the conditioned reinforcer continues to increase, but less and less rapidly. A point is reached beyond which further increases in frequency of reinforcement in the presence of the conditioned reinforcer bring

about only negligible increases in the rate of responding that is maintained by presentations of the conditioned reinforcer.

2. The schedule of presentations of the stimulus on which the conditioned reinforcer is based also helps determine its potency. This phenomenon is discussed in Chapter 6.

3. In a chain, a conditioned reinforcer is less potent the greater its distance from the primary reinforcement. Distance is measured in terms of either time or the number of links. Other factors being equal, the organism encounters conditioned reinforcers of greater and greater potency as it works its way through the chain.

4. The potency of a conditioned reinforcer also depends on the prevailing degree of motivation relevant to the primary reinforcer on which it is ultimately based. For example, conditioned reinforcers based on reinforcement by food are relatively weak when the organism has been recently well fed and relatively more powerful when the organism has been deprived of food.

Generalized Conditioned Reinforcers

It is possible to gain a degree of independence from the factors affecting the potency of a conditioned reinforcer by forming conditioned reinforcers based on two, several, or many primary reinforcers. In such cases, the conditioned reinforcer gains its potency from all of the reinforcers on which it is based. Such a stimulus is called a *generalized conditioned reinforcer*, to indicate the generality of its potency. Money, for example, owes its potency as a reinforcer to the wide range of primary and conditioned reinforcers on which it is based.

We will have many opportunities to apply these considerations about conditioned reinforcement in the next two chapters, which treat schedules of reinforcement.

six

Simple schedules
of positive reinforcement

As we have said before, it is by no means necessary to reinforce every occurrence of a response in order to increase or maintain the rate of responding. In fact, if continuous reinforcement were the only case ever studied, procedures and results of great interest would never have been discovered and developed, and since reinforcement outside of the laboratory is almost never continuous, nearly all applicability of the concept of reinforcement under natural conditions would be lost. A baby cries many times before one of its cries brings an attentive mother. We try many approaches before solving a difficult problem. A small boy may ask for lunch many times without success; but when a certain period of time has elapsed since breakfast, his request is granted. In each of these instances, only one occurrence of a response is reinforced and many are not. In the cases of crying and solving a problem, a number of unreinforced responses occur before one of them is reinforced, even though that number varies from occasion to occasion. In the case of asking for lunch, it must be lunchtime before a response is reinforced; the number of responses is relatively unimportant.

SCHEDULES OF INTERMITTENT REINFORCEMENT

Whenever the environment reinforces some but not all occurrences of a response emitted by the organism, a schedule of intermittent reinforcement is operating. Under *intermittent reinforcement*, only selected occurrences of a response are reinforced. The schedule of reinforcement is the rule followed by the environment—in an experiment, by the apparatus—in determining which among the many occurrences of a response will be reinforced.

Schedules of reinforcement have regular, orderly, and profound effects on the organism's rate of responding. The importance of schedules of reinforcement cannot be overestimated. No description, account, or explanation of any operant behavior of any organism is complete unless the schedule of reinforcement is specified. Schedules are the mainsprings of behavioral control, and thus the study of schedules is central to the study of behavior. Every reinforcer occurs according to some schedule, although many schedules are so complicated that ingenuity, insight, and experimental analysis are needed to formulate them precisely. The effort is worth-while, however, because the rate of responding can usually be more exactly controlled by manipulating the schedule of reinforcement than by any other method. Behavior that has been attributed to the supposed drives, needs, expectations, ruminations, or insights of the organism can often be related much more exactly to regularities produced by schedules of reinforcement. Many apparently erratic shifts in the rate of responding, which had formerly been ascribed to nebulous motivational variables or to "free will," have been traced by experiment to the influence of schedules of reinforcement.

Ratio and Interval Schedules

Simple schedules of reinforcement can be classified into two types: ratio schedules and interval schedules. *Ratio schedules* prescribe that a certain number of responses be emitted before one response is reinforced. The term *ratio* refers to the ratio of the total number of responses to the one reinforced response. With a ratio of 50 to 1, for example, an organism must emit 49 unreinforced responses preceding each reinforced response. *Interval schedules* prescribe that a given interval of time elapse before a response can be reinforced. The relevant interval can be measured from any event, but the end of the previous reinforcement is usually used.

Under ratio schedules the amount of time the organism takes to emit the necessary number of responses is irrelevant, while under interval schedules the number of responses is irrelevant so long as the organism emits the one response necessary for reinforcement after the interval has elapsed. Interval schedules have a built-in safety factor which is absent in ratio schedules: If the number of responses required by a ratio schedule is too high, the animal may never emit enough responses for reinforcement, and responding may extinguish. The residual level of responding under extinction may then be too low to produce reinforcement. Under interval schedules, however, the mere passage of time brings an opportunity for reinforcement; as long as the interval has elapsed, only a single response is needed for reinforcement. This single reinforcement, then, increases the rate of responding and ensures that responding will not be extinguished.

Variable and Fixed Schedules

Ratio and interval schedules can themselves be classified into two types: variable and fixed. When a *variable-ratio* schedule is operating, the number of responses required for one reinforcement varies from reinforcement to reinforcement in an irregular, but usually repeating, fashion. A typical sequence might reinforce the tenth response, then the hundredth, then the fiftieth, and continue following these numbers of responses: 5, 30, 150, 15, 40, 90, 210. Then, after ten more responses, the sequence would repeat and work through the same series of numbers over and over again until the session ended.

The value of a variable-ratio schedule is summarized by the average number of responses per reinforcement, here 70. For convenience, variable-ratio schedules are abbreviated as VR, and a number following the abbreviation indicates the average value of the ratios. In this way, the schedule described above is designated VR 70.

A *fixed-ratio* schedule, on the other hand, consistently requires the same total number of responses for every reinforced response. Fixed-ratio schedules are abbreviated FR. A fixed-ratio schedule requiring a total of 50 responses for each reinforced response is designated FR 50.

Similarly, a *variable-interval* (VI) schedule varies the amount of time that must elapse before a response can be reinforced. A *fixed-interval* (FI) schedule holds the required lapse of time constant.

The basis of all known schedules of positive reinforcement, no matter how complicated, can be reduced to variations of ratio and interval requirements, sometimes in combination with differential reinforcement of particular properties of responding, such as pausing or high rates. In this chapter, we will examine only the four elementary ratio and interval schedules — VR, FR, VI, and FI. We will discuss some of the more complicated cases in Chapter 7.

CHARACTERISTIC PERFORMANCES: ACQUISITION AND MAINTENANCE

Each schedule of reinforcement produces a characteristic performance. Depending on the schedule involved, the performance may consist of a steady, predictable rate of responding or of regular, oscillating, and predictable changes in rate. The appearance of this characteristic maintained performance is preceded by a period of *acquisition,* which occurs when the animal's responding is first reinforced according to the schedule. Although performance during acquisition is also regular and predictable, it differs from the maintained performance. During acquisition, the performance is always changing; but gradually, it comes closer and closer to the final maintained performance on the schedule. For example, when one schedule is terminated and replaced by another schedule, the maintained performance of the first schedule gradually changes, through a transition period, to the maintained performance of the second.

When a maintained performance on a schedule is followed by a period in which reinforcement is withdrawn entirely and responding extinguishes, the course and character of the extinction are to a very large extent determined by the preceding schedule of reinforcement. The following review of the simple schedules of reinforcement describes the performances typical of the various schedules and analyzes the variables which have been shown to determine the behavior in each case. A discussion of extinction following reinforcement on the four simple schedules follows later in this chapter.

Some Examples of Schedules of Reinforcement

Before describing and analyzing the performance maintained by each of the simple schedules of reinforcement, it may be helpful to point out some of the more common examples of schedules with which many readers will already be familiar. Behavior is reinforced on a fixed-ratio schedule in any factory that pays its employees on a piecework system. Payment depends on how much work is accomplished: each time a fixed number of items has been manufactured or serviced, the amount of the payment increases. Most workers work quite rapidly when they are working. But there is usually a pause, or breather, before beginning each block of work. This behavior is typical of that generated by fixed-ratio schedules.

True fixed-interval schedules, in which the length of the interval between reinforced responses does not vary at all, are difficult to find outside of the laboratory. However, there are numerous approximations. One is the workday, whose duration is relatively constant. Preparations for leaving the office, for example, increase in frequency as the time to leave draws nearer. It is not altogether clear in this case, however, whether the reinforcing stimulus is the departure from the office or the arrival at home.

Reinforcement on a variable-interval schedule is exemplified by trying to reach a busy person on the telephone. In this case, the behavior is the telephoning, and the reinforcer is hearing the person's voice instead of a busy signal. The schedule of reinforcement involves intervals because time is required for the person to stop talking and hang up so that you can get through to him. The intervals are variable because of the variable lengths of conversations on the telephone.

The best example of a variable-ratio schedule is the operation of the one-armed bandit, or slot machine. The machines may pay off every hundred plays on the average, but there are occasional instances of two successive winning plays and many instances of more than one hundred plays between pay-offs. The extremely high rate of responding and the persistence of many gamblers in playing these machines is typical of the behavior generated by variable-ratio schedules of reinforcement.

Performance on Variable-Ratio vs. Variable-Interval Schedules

The effects of variable-ratio and variable-interval schedules are vastly different. During maintenance, VR schedules produce very high and nearly constant rates of responding, sometimes approaching the physical capabilities of the organism. The rate may go as high as fifteen responses per second in a pigeon. VI schedules also produce nearly constant rates of responding, but the rates are usually of lower values than those produced by VR schedules.

Yoked Experimental Chambers

The difference between the performances maintained by the VR and the VI schedules and some of the reasons behind this difference are illustrated in the following experiment, which utilizes an arrangement known as *yoked experimental chambers*. In one experimental chamber, the key pecking of a pigeon is reinforced on a VR schedule. In another, completely isolated chamber, a key-peck of a second pigeon is reinforced whenever the first pigeon's response is reinforced. Only after the first pigeon emits the number of pecks required for reinforcement on the VR schedule will the next key-peck of the second pigeon be reinforced. In this way, the two birds receive the same number of reinforcements and receive them almost simultaneously. The difference is that while the first bird is reinforced on a VR schedule, the second bird is reinforced on a VI schedule: its reinforcement depends not on the number of its own pecks but on

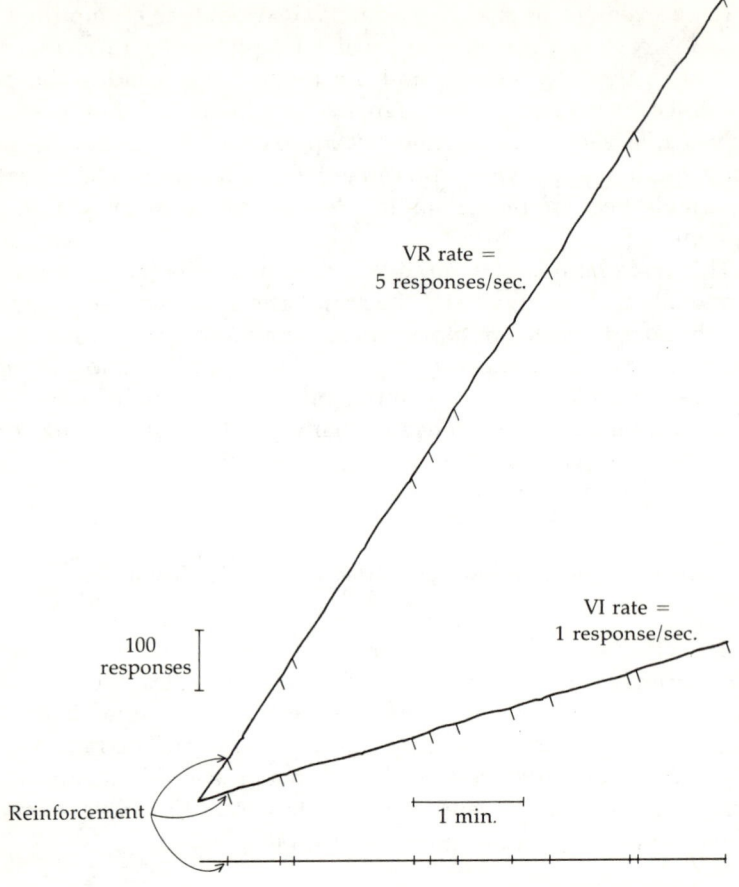

Figure 6.1 An illustration of the performance generated by variable-ratio and variable-interval schedules programed in yoked experimental chambers.

how long it takes the first bird to emit the number of responses required by the ratio. Thus, by using yoked experimental chambers, it is possible to hold the timing and frequency of reinforcement constant and to compare directly the other effects of VR and VI schedules of reinforcement.

After sufficient exposure to this procedure, the performance of each bird stabilizes in the form shown in Figure 6.1. Both birds exhibit a nearly constant rate of responding. However, the first bird, on the VR schedule, has a rate nearly five times as fast as the second bird, on the VI schedule. It is not surprising that both birds peck, since the pecking of each is reinforced. But what is responsible for the difference in rate and for the apparent stability of both rates of responding over time?

Since both birds' pecks are reinforced at approximately the same time, the difference in rate must be caused in some way by the interaction between the schedule and the behavior. Two factors of importance are the differential reinforcement of interresponse times and the relation between how rapidly the bird pecks and how often its pecks are reinforced.

Differential reinforcement of interresponse times. One aspect of the interaction between behavior and the schedule of reinforcement involves interresponse times, or IRTs. An *interresponse time* is simply the amount of time that passes between two responses. Except for the first response, every response in a sequence terminates the interresponse time measured from the previous response. Thus, a response comes at the end of the interresponse time with which it is associated. For example, if a pigeon pauses a relatively long time between two pecks on the key, the second peck is said to have a long interresponse time. If the pigeon waits a short time between pecks on the key, the second peck is said to have a short interresponse time.

Any sequence of responses can be described not only in terms of the rate at which the responses occur but also in terms of the interresponse times which make up the sequence. It is possible simply to list the values of each IRT in the sequence. Usually, however, we settle for a description in terms of the number of IRTs of various durations in the sequence—that is to say, a frequency distribution of IRTs.

The rate of responding and the IRTs of a sequence of responses are clearly related. Long IRTs are associated with low rates of responding; short IRTs, with high rates of responding. A sequence of responses at a high rate will contain relatively many short IRTs; a sequence of responses at a low rate will contain relatively many longer IRTs.

The IRT of a response is a characteristic that can be modified by selective reinforcement in the same way that the topography—the form, force, and duration—of a response can be modified (as discussed in Chapter 3). If we reinforce only those responses which come at the end of short IRTs, we find that short IRTs soon come to predominate in the performance, making for a high rate of responding. If we reinforce only those responses that come at the end of long IRTs, we soon find a low rate of responding characterized by long IRTs. Rate of responding is thus influenced by the differential reinforcement of IRTs. The VR schedule produces a higher rate than the VI because the VR differentially reinforces relatively short IRTs while the VI differentially reinforces relatively long IRTs.

Differential reinforcement of IRTs is a contingency arranged by the schedule of reinforcement. It occurs whenever it is more likely that the reinforced responses will occur at the end of relatively long or relatively short IRTs. When the schedule is such that the reinforced responses in a sequence of responses tend to occur at the end of the shorter IRTs in the sequence, the shorter IRTs will be differentially reinforced. This is what happens on a VR schedule, and the result is a tendency toward shorter IRTs and, hence, higher rates of responding. The VI schedule, on the other hand, differentially reinforces relatively long IRTs because the reinforced responses in a sequence will predominantly be those that terminate the longer IRTs in the sequence. This results in a tendency toward longer IRTs and, hence, lower rates of responding.

Differential reinforcement of IRTs is possible because an organism's IRTs are variable rather than constant. A typical sequence is indicated in Figure 6.2. As the organism begins to respond under any schedule of reinforcement, it emits a sequence of variable IRTs that includes groups of responses occurring more closely together than others. These groups are called *bursts*, and they are indicated by the brackets in Figure 6.2. When a VI schedule interacts with such a sequence of varying IRTs, the chances that any one response will be reinforced are greater the longer its IRT. For example, in the experiment with yoked chambers, as time passes, the bird on the VR is emitting more and more responses. The more responses it emits, the greater the chances that it will reach the number of responses required for reinforcement on the VR, which will in turn make reinforcement immediately available to the bird on the VI. Thus, the longer the bird on the VI schedule waits to emit each response, the more likely it is that the bird on the VR will have satisfied his ratio and, hence, the more likely it is that the response will be reinforced. Similarly, in an ordinary VI schedule programed only by time, the longer the IRT, the greater the chances that the interval required by the schedule will have ended. This differential reinforcement of long IRTs helps keep the rate of responding on VI schedules relatively low.

On a VR schedule, differential reinforcement of short IRTs comes about because it is more likely that one of a burst of several responses will be reinforced than that the first response in the burst will be reinforced. Reinforcement on the VR schedule depends, of course, on the number of responses emitted. Now, because bursts of responses involve many responses, the chances that the number of responses required for reinforcement will be reached by one of the later responses in a burst are greater than the chances that the first response in the burst will reach the required number. And the later responses in a burst, of course, have shorter IRTs than the first re-

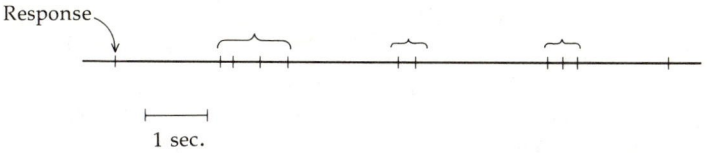

Figure 6.2 A sequence of interresponse times. The brackets indicate bursts of responses.

sponse in the burst. Thus, the shorter IRTs are differentially reinforced. The result is the high rate of responding typically produced by VR schedules.

The effects of differential reinforcement of IRTs can be demonstrated experimentally by making two simple modifications of the schedule of reinforcement. These modifications arrange for the explicit differential reinforcement of IRTs. They can be added to any schedule; here, however, we will use the VI schedule.

The first modification restricts the value of the reinforced IRTs: in order to be reinforced, a response must have an IRT that falls within certain limits of duration. This modification is made by hooking a schedule that limits the reinforced IRTs onto the VI schedule. Whenever one schedule is hooked onto the end of another, the resulting compound schedule is called a *tandem schedule.*

A tandem schedule built on a VI schedule is developed by first establishing performance on the VI schedule alone and then adding the additional requirement, here the requirement restricting the length of the IRTs. There is no change in stimulus when one schedule is added to the other. After the next interval of the VI ends, the first response is not reinforced as usual; instead, reinforcement is withheld until the organism emits a response having an IRT of the required length. When an IRT is long or short enough, its terminal response is reinforced, and the next interval of the VI schedule begins.

After the restricting requirement is added and the second part of the tandem schedule begins, there is usually an initial decrease in the frequency of reinforcement because a reinforceable IRT usually does not occur immediately. Then, because of the differential reinforcement of IRTs, the rate of responding increases if the required IRT is shorter than that usually emitted on the VI schedule or the rate decreases if the required IRT is longer than usual.

A second modification, which affects the differential reinforcement of short IRTs, is the limited hold. With an ordinary VI schedule, once reinforcement becomes available with the termination of each required interval, it remains available until the next response occurs and is reinforced. With a limited hold, however, the reinforcement remains available only for a definite, usually short, period of time. This period of time is called the *limited hold*. If no response occurs during the limited hold, there is no reinforcement and the next interval of the VI schedule begins. Thus, if the organism does not respond quickly enough, reinforcement is no longer available. A short limited hold functions to produce an increased rate of responding.

The explicit modifications that are arranged by tandem schedules and the limited hold offer proof that differential reinforcement of IRTs does indeed influence the rate of responding. The effects of differential reinforcement of IRTs account for much of the character of the performances produced by various schedules of reinforcement. The performances are complicated, however, and a single factor can offer only a partial explanation. All of the factors contributing to a performance or to part of a performance on a schedule need to be investigated before the performance can be thoroughly understood. Differential reinforcement of IRTs is a major factor in determining the rates of responding on VR and VI schedules, but it is not the only one.

Rate of responding and rate of reinforcement. A second factor affecting characteristic performance is the relation between the rate of responding and the rate of reinforcement: when the rate of reinforcement is dependent on the rate of responding, the rate of responding tends to be higher. This is the case on the VR schedule where the faster the organism emits its ratio, the faster reinforcement comes. The resulting higher rate of responding, in turn, makes shorter IRTs available for differential reinforcement. Thus, in the case of the VR, the dependence of rate of reinforcement on rate of responding and the differential reinforcement of short IRTs have an additive effect resulting in extremely high rates of responding.

On a VI schedule, higher rates of responding do not result in more frequent reinforcement, but extremely low rates may result in a lower frequency of reinforcement by causing significantly long delays between the availability of reinforcement and the reinforced response. Only at very low rates of responding, therefore, does the correlation between the rates of responding and reinforcement tend to affect the rate of responding on a VI schedule. This fact, in combination with the differential reinforcement of relatively long IRTs, helps maintain moderate rates of responding on VI schedules.

Factors Influencing Stability of Responding on VR and VI Schedules

There are several factors responsible for the stability of the rates of responding on VI and VR schedules. One of these involves the actual values of the intervals and ratios composing the schedules: if the range and distribution of the ratios or intervals are within certain limits, stability is maintained. These limits are not well defined at present, but it is known that the sequence of intervals or ratios should be carefully chosen so that neither time nor number is consistently correlated with reinforcement or nonreinforcement. This means that an acceptable sequence must include a proper balance ranging from very short to long intervals or ratios, without any systematic patterning in the sequence. In short, the ability of VI and VR schedules to maintain stable rates of responding depends on their variable nature; a stable rate of responding will be maintained as long as the organism is not required to go too long without reinforcement and as long as no discriminable feature of the schedule reliably precedes the occurrence or nonoccurrence of reinforcement.

Once a stable performance has been established, two factors make it resistant to change. First, the behavior involved in responding at a constant rate becomes a conditioned reinforcer because it is present at the time of reinforcement. As a conditioned reinforcer, responding at a constant rate reinforces the behavior which results in its occurrence, and that behavior is precisely the emission of responses at the constant rate. Thus, constancy itself becomes reinforcing. Second, responding at a constant rate is superstitiously maintained. Although it is certainly not required by the schedule for reinforcement, responding at a constant rate is nevertheless reinforced, because it is the only rate emitted by the organism and it thus prevails at the time of reinforcement.

Effects of Changes in the Value of the Ratio
or Interval on VR and VI Schedules

At almost all ratio values, VR schedules will produce the characteristic high, stable rate. However, beyond certain values, the range and distribution of the ratios comprising the schedule become crucially important. Individual ratios of greater than a certain value result in abrupt pauses in responding. Pauses also occur if not enough short and medium ratios are included in the schedule. Naturally, pauses both lower the rate of responding and disturb the stable nature of the performance.

Abrupt pauses in the normally smooth and rapid rate of responding on a ratio schedule are referred to as *strain*. Strain usually occurs when the value of the ratio is increased too rapidly in an experiment. It is possible to maintain responding on ratio schedules of extremely high values provided that the value is approached slowly from lower values. If the value of the ratio is increased too rapidly, the performance may exhibit strain. The strain disappears, however, if a lower value of the ratio is reinstated. Thereafter, higher and higher ratios may be obtained if care is taken to advance the value of the ratio slowly enough to avoid strain.

The lengths of the intervals comprising a VI schedule (and, hence, the rate of reinforcement provided by the schedule) have a profound influence on the rate of responding. For pigeons, as the rate of reinforcement increases from zero (extinction) to about fifty per hour, the rate of responding increases rapidly from nearly zero to about one response per second. Beyond fifty reinforcements per hour, the rate of responding increases very slowly.

The range and distribution of the intervals comprising VI schedules exert precise control over the moment-to-moment rate of responding. Changes in rate at any time in the performance can be predicted with excellent accuracy from nothing more than the frequency distribution of the lengths of the intervals in the schedule and the overall rate of responding maintained by the schedule. Unfortunately, the details of how to make such predictions are beyond the scope of a primer.

Performance on Fixed-Ratio Schedules

A stable maintained performance on a fixed-ratio schedule develops rapidly, particularly if the ratio is small. What constitutes a small ratio depends on the animal involved. A small ratio for the rat is about ten or fifteen. For the pigeon, a ratio of fifty is small. Responding on extremely high ratios, on the order of two thousand for the pigeon, has been developed by starting with a small ratio and gradually increasing it over a course of time.

The typical FR performance, shown in Figure 6.3, is characterized by a high rate of responding which is sustained from the first response after reinforcement up to the last reinforced response. On small ratios, there is no pause after reinforcement; in fact, the organism occasionally continues to respond during the presentation of the reinforcer. Evidently FR schedules generate such a high tendency to respond that the bird would rather peck than eat. On high ratios, again at different values depending on the organism, there is a pause after reinforcement, followed by an essentially instantaneous transition into the typical high rate as soon as responding resumes.

Factors Influencing the FR Performance

The occurrence of a high and constant rate of responding on the FR schedule depends on the same factors as does performance on the

VR: differential reinforcement of relatively short IRTs, the dependence of the rate of reinforcement on the rate of responding, and the establishment of the prevailing rate as a conditioned reinforcer by virtue of its association with reinforcement.

Additional factors that influence the performance on the FR arise from the constant number of responses required for reinforcement. One of these factors is that the period of time between reinforcements —that is, the time it takes the organism to complete the ratio—is relatively constant. This establishes the occurrence of reinforcement as a stimulus associated with a period of nonreinforcement. This period is longer and, hence, more discriminable the larger the ratio. The effect is a pause in responding after each reinforcement when the value of the ratio is sufficiently large.

As long as the ratio is kept small, however, the fixed nature of the schedule will contribute to the stability of responding, since the number of responses emitted becomes a discriminative stimulus.

Figure 6.3 The performance generated by two different fixed-ratio schedules.

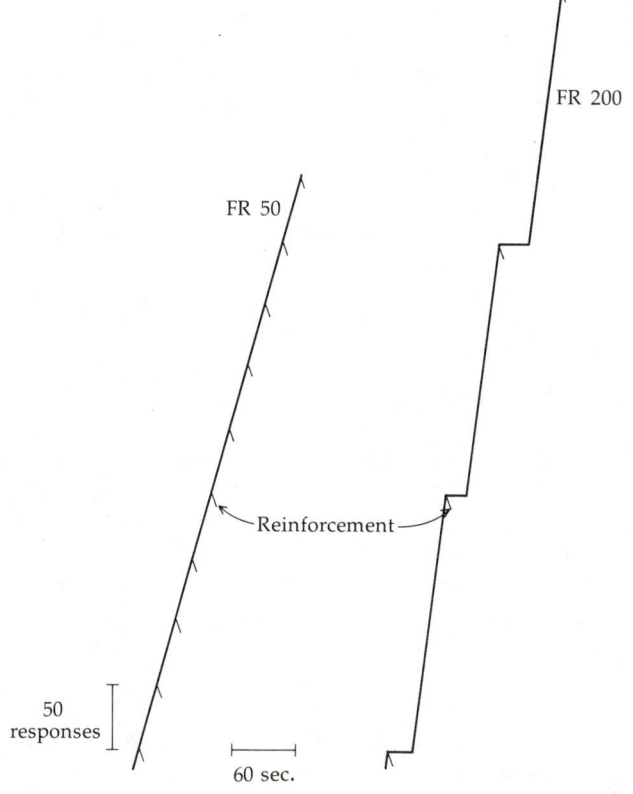

This is the essence of performance on the FR schedule: Each response brings the number of responses emitted one step closer to the number in the presence of which a response is reinforced. Each response becomes a conditioned reinforcer of the previous response and a discriminative stimulus for the next. The sequence of responses within each ratio is thus a chain, which runs off at a constant rate after the first response.

Mixed Schedules

The FR performance raises an interesting aside, since it implies that the organism can count its responses. "Counting" here is different from subitizing, which is the immediate discrimination of the number of objects in a group. Some birds, for example, can discriminate between groups of up to about seven objects solely on the basis of their number. Counting, however, occurs with some degree of accuracy at least up into the hundreds.

For example, in the following procedure, which involves what is called a *mixed schedule* of reinforcement, the number of responses emitted since the last reinforcement functions as a discriminative stimulus that occasions pausing. A pigeon is subjected to a schedule such that after each reinforcement, the ratio for the next reinforcement will be either 100 or 750. Each ratio occurs half the time, and there is no exteroceptive discriminative stimulus or any other means of predicting which ratio is in effect. Lacking an exteroceptive discriminative stimulus to distinguish between the two ratios, the organism uses the only stimulus that is available: the number of responses it has emitted since the previous reinforcement. Thus, after each reinforcement, a short pause appropriate to the FR 100 occurs, followed by somewhat more than 100 responses at a rate also appropriate to the FR 100. If the pigeon's hundreth response has not been reinforced (that is, if the FR 750 is in effect), a pause appropriate to the FR 750 soon ensues, followed by pecking at a rate appropriate to the FR 750. The fact that the pigeon will usually emit from 110 to 150 responses before pausing may indicate something of its capacity to discriminate number. The second pause is occasioned by the discriminative stimuli provided by at least 100 pecks and no reinforcement, since those are the stimuli differentially associated with the FR 750.

Performance on Fixed-Interval Schedules

Performance on fixed-interval schedules can best be understood by tracing the development of this performance from that maintained by a variable-interval schedule. Suppose that a VI schedule is changed to an FI of ten minutes per interval. The next reinforced response will be the first response that occurs after ten minutes have passed since the last reinforced response. As one ten-minute interval follows another, the rate of responding at first continues to be about the same as it was on the VI. Gradually, however, the rate of responding just after reinforcement declines and the rate just before reinforcement increases. The decline is owing to the consistent lack of reinforcement during the early part of the fixed interval. As with FR schedules using large ratios, the occurrence of reinforcement becomes a discriminative stimulus associated with the succeeding period of nonreinforcement.

Thus, on an FI schedule, the organism forms a discrimination in the same way that it forms other discriminations (see Chapter 4). Because the development of the FI performance is essentially a discrimination process, the overall rate toward the end of each interval increases over what it was during the VI. This increase in rate is owing, at least in part, to behavioral contrast (also discussed in Chapter 4). Responding extinguishes in the presence of the stimulus associated with nonreinforcement (the early part of the interval), and the rate of responding increases in the presence of the stimulus associated with reinforcement (the later part of the interval). The typical performance maintained by an FI schedule is known as the *FI scallop*. Figure 6.4 shows the characteristic pause and accelerated responding within each fixed interval.

Figure 6.4 The performance generated by a one-minute fixed-interval schedule.

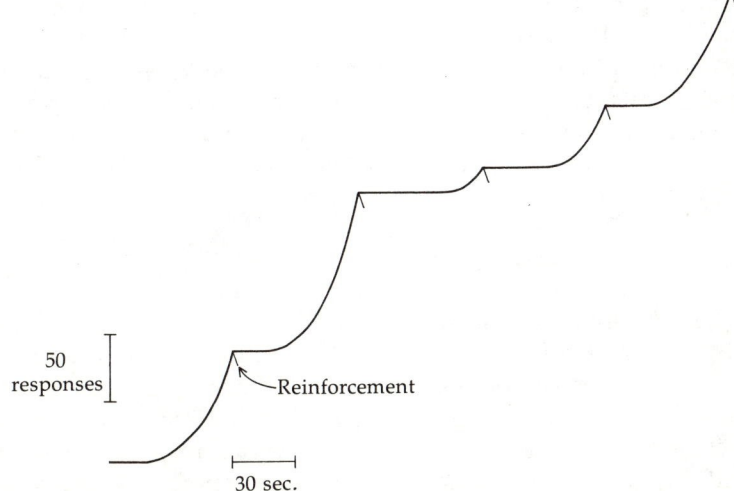

50 responses

Reinforcement

30 sec.

The most striking difference between FI and FR performances is that the FI performance accelerates in rate from the first response following one reinforcement up to the terminal rate before the next reinforcement. The FR performance, on the other hand, although it may have a pause following reinforcement, always has the same high rate whenever the organism is responding (see Figure 6.3).

One reason for this difference is that the chaining of responses which promotes stability of responding on the FR does not occur on the FI. Since the number of responses is irrelevant on the FI, number does not become a discriminative stimulus or a conditioned reinforcer; thus, chaining never occurs. Rather, the organism is controlled by its temporal discrimination.

The accelerated responding on the FI, which replaces the steady rate observed on the FR, can be attributed in part to generalization; the FI scallop is, in fact, a kind of gradient of generalization (discussed in Chapter 4). The rate of responding increases through the interval as the properties of the discriminative stimuli in the animal's environment more and more closely approximate the properties of the stimuli actually present when reinforcement is delivered. In the case of the FI, as the temporal stimulus comes closer to the actual stimulus associated with reinforcement—that is, as the passage of time approaches the actual time when reinforcement has been delivered—the rate of responding increases. To complicate matters, the gradual increase in rate, an aspect of the organism's own behavior, also may become a conditioned reinforcer.

After an organism has been exposed to a fixed-interval schedule of reinforcement for a relatively long time, the character of its performance sometimes changes to resemble that generated by a fixed-ratio, with a considerable pause after reinforcement at the beginning of each interval. The reason for this seems to be that, by chance, the same number of responses has occurred in each of several successive intervals. Thus, one of the most powerful contingencies arranged by fixed-ratio schedules is sometimes simulated on the FI and takes hold of the behavior to generate a performance like that generated by a fixed-ratio schedule.

Other Effects of FI Schedules

The increased tendency to engage in the response as the end of the fixed interval approaches is associated with a decreased tendency to engage in other, competing responses. If the organism can run and move about in an open area or a wheel in between pecks or bar-presses, it does so less and less as the interval progresses. Also, if a second response is concurrently available and reinforced on a different schedule, for example an FR, the organism's tendency to emit that response decreases as the interval progresses: FR performances of the second response occur regularly in the early part of each interval but fail to occur later in the intervals. We reflect this sort of change in our own behavior when we say that we have something more important to do.

Concomitant with these changes, and perhaps causing them, is an increase in the strength of the control exerted over the response by the discriminative stimuli present when the response is reinforced on the FI schedule. Suppose that two response keys, left and right, are always available to a pigeon. One of them is always red and one green, but the side on which each color appears changes with each peck on either key. Thus, sometimes the left key is red and the right green, while the rest of the time the left key is green and the right red. The schedule is an FI. The reinforced response is a peck on the red key, whether that key is on the left or the right. In this instance, the total rate of pecking on the two keys increases during each interval, as it normally does in an FI schedule. However, as the end of each interval approaches, the proportion of the total number of pecks on the red key increases. When pecking first begins, there are about as many pecks on the red as on the green key. Near the end of the interval, however, the bird pecks almost exclusively on the red key, even though it must switch from one key to the other to do so. The strength of control over the response by the particular aspect of the key associated with reinforcement – its red color – increases throughout the interval.

The intensifying of stimulus control as the interval draws to a close may also be seen in a procedure called *matching to sample*. In matching to sample, a response is reinforced if it is made to a stimulus which is the same as another stimulus. Specifically, the organism faces three keys, each of which can be either red or green. One is lighted, and when it is pecked, the other two keys are lighted, only one of which is the same color as the first key. A peck on the key that is the same color as the first key is reinforced. Then the sequence is repeated.

Several interesting variations of this procedure are possible. One is to expand the number of choices by increasing the number of stimuli from which the matching stimulus is selected. Another is to introduce delays between the presentation of the sample and the presentation of the choices in order to study memory. In this case, the sample is turned off when pecked, and the choices are turned on only after a delay.

Another variation, of particular interest to us in this chapter, is the application of schedules of reinforcement to the matching.

Matching may, for example, be reinforced on a fixed-ratio schedule, whereby every nth correct match is reinforced. This serves to increase the rate at which matching takes place and, unexpectedly, the accuracy with which the organism matches.

The variables of rate and accuracy of matching are strikingly manipulated by a fixed-interval schedule. For example, when reinforcement occurs only after the first correct match after three minutes have elapsed since the last reinforcement, the rate of matching shows the same FI scallop as has just been described for an ordinary FI performance. The result of considerable importance for education is that the accuracy of matching steadily improves during the interval. Errors tend to be limited to the early part of the interval, when responding is not frequent. Toward the end of the interval, when matching is proceeding at a rapid rate, the organism almost never makes an incorrect match.

EXTINCTION AFTER MAINTENANCE
ON THE FOUR SIMPLE SCHEDULES

When responses are no longer reinforced, the rate of responding eventually approaches zero. The usual course of extinction for each of the four simple schedules is shown in Figure 6.5. Behavior maintained on the four simple schedules is more resistant to extinction than behavior maintained by continuous reinforcement. As the figure illustrates, the transition between the maintained performance and the extremely low rate characteristic of extinction is different depending on the previous schedule of reinforcement.

After reinforcement on an FI schedule, responding during the first interval of extinction is normal, except that the high terminal rate continues beyond the end of the interval, when reinforcement would have occurred. In a short time, responding ceases abruptly. Then, after a pause, there is a period of acceleration, followed by the original terminal rate, which is again followed by an abrupt end to responding. This pattern of pause, respond, accelerate, and abruptly stop, whose origins can be seen in the scallop of the maintained performance, continues throughout extinction. The pauses become longer and the periods of responding become shorter as the rate of responding approaches zero.

Extinction following FR reinforcement is also influenced by the previously maintained performance. It is characterized by abrupt pauses and by responding at the high rate that prevailed during reinforcement. Usually there are no intermediate rates. The overall rate of responding approaches zero as the pauses become longer and

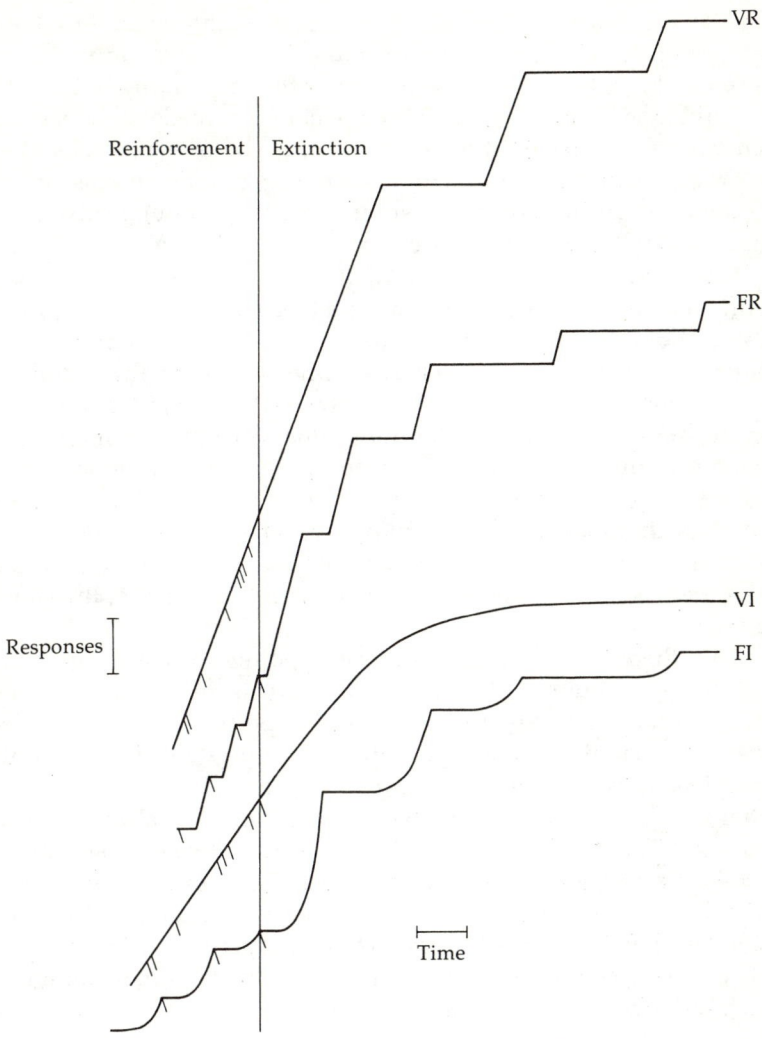

Figure 6.5 The general course and features of extinction following reinforcement on each of the four simple schedules.

the periods of responding become shorter. When the organism does respond, however, it responds at the former high rate.

After VR reinforcement, if the distribution of ratios has been judiciously chosen, a truly amazing number of responses at a high, sustained rate may be emitted during extinction. The transition toward a rate of zero occurs mainly through the occurrence of more and longer abrupt periods of nonresponding. Again, the high rate characteristic of the maintained performance usually occurs whenever the organism is responding. The lack of intermediate rates of responding during extinction after ratio schedules is additional evidence for the tightly chained character of the responding in the ratio.

Extinction following VI reinforcement proceeds as a steadily decreasing rate of responding without abrupt pauses. Typically, there are variations in the local rate of responding, but the decrease in rate is monotonic if the rate is measured over long enough intervals of time (usually thirty seconds or one minute is long enough).

One theory, which was born of the experimenter's desire to predict the speed of extinction, says that extinction is more rapid the greater the difference between the conditions prevailing during extinction and during maintenance. One source of this similarity theory of extinction was the observation that the rapidity of extinction depends somewhat on the distribution of ratios or intervals in the maintenance schedule. Roughly speaking—and it is at best only a rough theory—the more long ratios or intervals of unreinforced responses there are in the maintenance schedule, the more slowly extinction proceeds. In other words, the more difficult the discrimination between the maintenance schedule and extinction, the slower the extinction.

This theory is important because it points to one of the variables—the distribution of ratios and intervals in the maintenance schedule—that affect extinction. It is also probably valid, since we know that changing other stimuli that were present during maintenance increases the speed of extinction. This effect was described earlier in Chapter 4 as one of the properties of generalization. If the theory is to approach adequacy, however, it will have to specify the effects on extinction of each effective parameter of the maintenance schedule. That is to say, it will have to define "similarity" in satisfactory, empirical detail—in terms of the properties of the schedules and of the behavior that are discriminable by the organism and to which the organism can be shown to attend.

seven

Multiple, compound, and concurrent schedules of reinforcement

In Chapter 6, we examined the performances characteristic of the four simple schedules of reinforcement: the fixed-ratio, the variable-ratio, the fixed-interval, and the variable-interval. In this chapter, we will examine some more complicated schedules of reinforcement. These schedules are built out of the same basic elements as the simpler schedules, and the performances they generate and maintain are the results of the same principles that regulate the performances on the simpler schedules of reinforcement.

MULTIPLE SCHEDULES OF REINFORCEMENT

We have already studied some multiple schedules of reinforcement and extinction in Chapter 4 in order to bring out some of the properties of discrimination and generalization. Technically, a *multiple schedule* consists of two or more independent schedules presented successively to the organism, each in the presence of a discriminable exteroceptive stimulus. Multiple schedules are mixed schedules with exteroceptive discriminative stimuli added. For example, a pigeon's key might be alternately lighted red, then green, and then blue, with reinforcement on an FI schedule when it is red and on a VR schedule when it is green and with no reinforcement (extinction) when it is blue. For convenience, the same response — pecking, for example — is usually reinforced or extinguished during each color, although a different response could be studied in the presence of each stimulus.

Each particular stimulus presented during a multiple schedule occasions a performance appropriate to the schedule of reinforcement associated with that stimulus. On the schedule described above, the organism's rate of responding forms an FI scallop while the red light is on. When the light changes to green, the rate smooths out into the high, steady rate appropriate to the VR. When the light turns blue, the performance moderates into the very low rate characteristic of extinction.

Although the performances typical of the individual schedules when they are used in isolation come to prevail when they are combined in multiple schedules, there are also interactions among the component schedules. An organism's performance at a given time under given conditions is in part determined by the performance and its consequences at other times and under other conditions. For example, a businessman's behavior in the evening is partly determined by what happened during the day at the office. In an experimental situation, the performance on a given schedule is slightly different in a multiple schedule than it is when that one schedule alone is presented to the organism. These differences are important, even though they are small in magnitude and the performance remains recognizably appropriate to the schedule.

The interactions among the component schedules are studied in two ways. A difference may be noted between the performance on a schedule when it is presented alone and when it is presented as one component of a multiple schedule; or a difference may be noted between the performances on the schedule used as a component in two or more different multiple schedules.

In a real sense, all behavior is reinforced on multiple schedules. Even in experimental work in the laboratory, a single schedule studied in daily sessions is only one component of a multiple schedule that also includes the schedule provided by the organism's living quarters. It is common to think of deprivation as the only relevant variable associated with the intersession period in the living quarters, but interactions between it and the schedule under study also may be important.

Interactions have usually been studied experimentally in the specialized case of a multiple schedule made up of two simple schedules. The same response and the same reinforcer are used in each component schedule. In cases like this, two kinds of interactions have been found.

First, the character of the performances may be changed, but never enough to distort seriously the performance typical of each schedule. For example, in a multiple schedule composed of an FI and an FR (a multiple FI-FR), there may be, during the FI, occurrences of

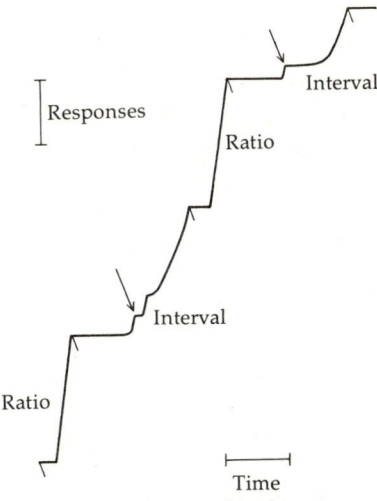

Figure 7.1 The performance on fixed-interval and fixed-ratio schedules when used as components in a multiple schedule. The arrows indicate one of the effects of the alternated ratio schedule on the performance on the interval schedule.

bursts of responding at the high rate appropriate to the FR, especially during the period of acceleration. Such bursts are illustrated in Figure 7.1. They do not occur during the typical FI performance when that schedule is used alone. This interaction does not, however, obscure the orderly progression of pause, acceleration, and high terminal rate that is typical of the FI.

The second type of interaction involves the overall rate of responding. The rate of responding on a given schedule will vary depending on the multiple schedule of which it is a component. The most prevalent interactions in terms of overall rate have already been discussed in Chapter 4 under the topics of generalization and behavioral contrast in a multiple schedule composed of reinforcement and extinction components.

COMPOUND SCHEDULES OF REINFORCEMENT

A *compound schedule* reinforces a single response according to the requirements of two or more schedules of reinforcement at the same time. Depending on the details of the compound schedule, an occurrence of the response may be reinforced when the requirements of *all* component schedules have been met, or when the requirements of *any one* of the schedules have been met, or when *any combination* of the requirements of two or more schedules have been met. There is thus a very large number of possible compound schedules.

Conjunctive Schedules

One of the most interesting compound schedules is the *conjunctive schedule,* in which the requirements of both (or all) of the schedules must be met before a response is reinforced. For example, in a conjunctive FI and FR schedule, a response is reinforced provided that both the fixed interval of time has elapsed since the last reinforced response *and* the fixed ratio of responses has been emitted. The performance on this conjunctive schedule looks like a combination of the performances usually generated by the FI and FR schedules separately. In each period of time between reinforcements, there is the pause and the acceleration of responding characteristic of an FI schedule. In addition, there is usually a period of responding at a very high rate, as on an FR schedule, somewhere in the middle of the interval. Following this, the lower rate and acceleration prevail once more. The organism fulfills the numerical requirement of the FR schedule during the period of responding at a high rate. The rest of the time, responding is appropriate to an FI schedule.

There is another interesting characteristic of this conjunctive schedule: it maintains a lower overall rate of responding than does a simple FI of the same duration. This characteristic appears if we change a simple FI schedule, which maintains a certain average rate of responding, into a conjunctive FI-FR by requiring that there be at least the number of responses specified by the FR in each interval in order for reinforcement to occur. The result is a lower overall rate of responding, perhaps because the FR requirement does not allow reinforcement to occur at the end of intervals containing small numbers of responses.

Diagrams of Schedules

In discussing complicated schedules of reinforcement, it is useful to have some means of visualizing them. A method of diagraming has been developed which uses a cumulative record of the responding whose reinforcement is to be scheduled. This method helps the experimenter to see exactly how the schedule and the responding interact, and it allows him to create new schedules simply by drawing symbols on the cumulative record.

Imagine that reinforcement has just occurred or the session has just begun and that the cumulative record is being drawn from its origin by the organism's responding as it occurs. The symbols that we draw on the cumulative record will indicate the point or points on the record that the cumulative curve must reach before the next occurrence of the response will be reinforced.

Figure 7.2 shows diagrams of various schedules. In graph 1 of the figure, the solid line drawn perpendicular to the time axis indicates that the next response to be reinforced will be the first response made after the cumulative record crosses that line at any point, regardless of how many responses have been emitted by then. The line itself represents a fixed period of time from the start of the record; the diagram therefore represents a fixed-interval schedule. Graph 2 of the figure represents a fixed-ratio schedule of reinforcement: after the record reaches the fixed height indicated by the solid line, regardless of how much time it takes, the next response will be reinforced.

Thus, a solid line indicates that a response will be reinforced once the cumulative record crosses that line. The location of the line along the abscissa or the ordinate determines the value of the FI or the FR, respectively. In graph 1, for example, since the line intersects the time axis at a point whose distance from the origin represents fifteen seconds, the schedule is an FI 15 seconds. Likewise, in graph 2, the distance of the line from the origin represents fifteen responses, and the schedule is an FR 15.

It is conventional to draw a short line at an angle through the longer line to indicate a variable requirement of time or number. Graphs 3 and 4 in the figure are diagrams of variable-interval and variable-ratio schedules, respectively. The position of the longer line on its axis represents the *average* value of the variable-ratio or variable-interval schedule.

The conjunctive schedule discussed above is diagramed in graph 5 of the figure. Both schedules must be satisfied in order for a response to be reinforced; thus, the cumulative record must enter the shaded area bounded by both a temporal and a numerical criterion. Graph 6 of the figure represents a conjunctive schedule with a VI and an FR component.

Alternative Schedules

Other types of schedules emerge as different configurations of lines are drawn. For example, graph 7 represents an *alternative schedule* with an FI and an FR component. On this schedule, a response is reinforced when *either* the FI *or* the FR requirement has been satisfied, that is to say, after the cumulative record has crossed *either* the vertical *or* the horizontal line.

Interlocking Schedules

Graph 8 of Figure 7.2 shows one kind of *interlocking schedule*: a response is reinforced after a certain number of responses, but the

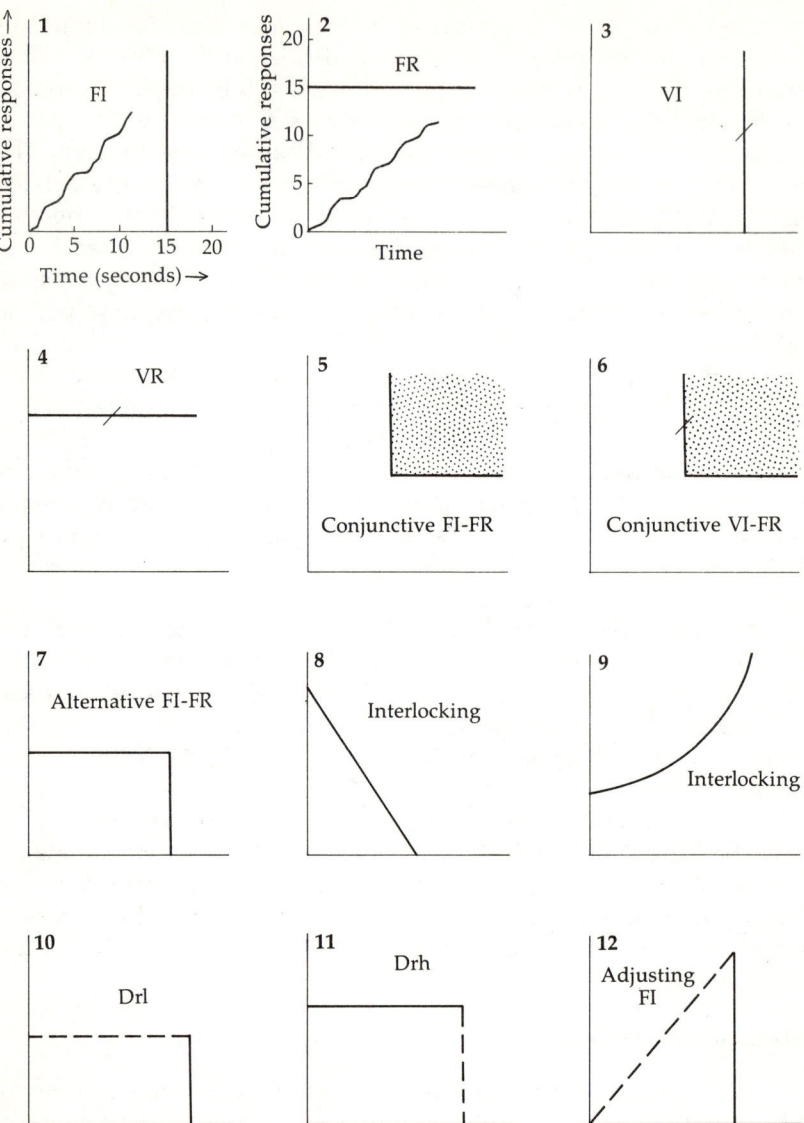

Figure 7.2 Diagrams of various schedules of reinforcement.

number decreases the longer the time since the last reinforced response. Graph 9 shows another interlocking schedule, one in which the number of responses increases the longer the time since the previous reinforcement.

The increasing interlocking schedule is particularly dangerous, since the requirement for reinforcement becomes prohibitively large after a short time. Thus, responding may never be reinforced if it does not begin at a high enough rate. If a group of organisms were subjected to this schedule, they would very rapidly separate into two distinct groups: those who initially responded rapidly enough to allow the schedule to maintain their responding and those who initially responded so slowly that reinforcement never occurred. The first group would continue to respond rapidly, and the latter group would soon not respond at all. This is the sort of insidious schedule that exists in cumulative educational systems in which, as time passes, the requirements for success become larger and larger. It is, for example, extremely difficult to perform well in the third grade if very little was learned in the first and second. Such an educational system develops and maintains a separation of students which appears to be dictated by nature but which actually depends primarily on their initial performance.

Drl and drh Schedules

If we add another symbol to those available for diagraming, other schedules emerge. For example, let a dashed line mean the following: if the cumulative record reaches this line, do *not* reinforce but begin the requirement again. Graph 10 of Figure 7.2 shows what happens when this symbol is added as a numerical limitation to the FI. A response is reinforced provided that sufficient time has elapsed since the previous reinforced response (or since the last time a line was crossed) *and* provided that *fewer* than the indicated number of responses has occurred. This schedule, which essentially limits the rate of responding that precedes the reinforced response, is important enough to have earned a separate name, *drl*, or differential reinforcement of low rates of responding.

If the dashed line is added as a temporal limitation to the FR, as in graph 11 of the figure, the schedule is called a *drh*, or differential reinforcement of high rates of responding. The response is reinforced provided that the indicated number of responses occurs before the indicated time elapses. The drh produces extraordinarily high rates of responding.

It is, of course, possible to generate even more complicated drl- and drh-like schedules. One of them is shown in graph 12. In this case, the value of the restriction on the number of responses emitted increases as time goes on. Thus, the organism may, by the end of the interval, emit as many responses as are indicated by the highest point on the dashed line and still be reinforced; but it will not be reinforced if it emits them too early in the interval.

The drl schedule has been studied extensively, particularly in the case in which the numerical limitation is set at one response. The one response is reinforced only if it occurs after the fixed interval of time has elapsed since the occurrence of the last response. If the response occurs too early, it is not reinforced and the required pause begins again. The fact that this is a pure case of selective reinforcement of interresponse times (IRTs) accounts for the great interest in this schedule.

In the usual drl schedule there is no upper limit on the length of the IRT. As long as the IRT is longer than the required time, it is reinforced. It is possible, however, to limit further the reinforced IRTs by adding a limited hold (see Chapter 6). In that case, only those responses are reinforced that terminate IRTs which are longer than a certain duration and shorter than a slightly longer duration.

The drl schedule generates a very low rate of responding; however, the rate is usually systematically higher than it would be if the IRTs were, in fact, always long enough for reinforcement. This means, of course, that there are many unreinforced responses. Although this phenomenon has not been empirically analyzed, it seems safe to guess that the higher rate occurs because responses are reinforced and perhaps because the organism does not consistently attend to the relevant stimulus, the duration of the IRT.

The structure of the performance on a drl schedule of reinforcement is clearly seen in a graph of the frequency with which IRTs of various lengths occur. Such a frequency distribution for a typical performance appears in Figure 7.3. In this case, the only responses reinforced were those that terminated IRTs at least ten seconds long; there was no upper limit on the length of the IRTs. The frequencies have been tabulated in class intervals, each two seconds long. As the graph illustrates, the frequency of short IRTs is lower than that of the longer reinforced IRTs. The distribution roughly resembles a gradient of generalization (see Chapter 4): except for the very short IRTs, the larger the difference between the duration of the IRT and the duration of the reinforced IRTs, the less frequently does the IRT occur. Although some short unreinforced IRTs do continue to occur, the organism's performance is nevertheless surprisingly precise, especially since most of the time it must measure time only from its previous response and not from an exteroceptive event.

Interresponse Times per Opportunity (IRTs/op)

Although Figure 7.3 shows a striking temporal discrimination, this way of examining the data does not give as much credit to the accuracy of the performance as it deserves. A comparison of long and short IRTs in terms of their frequency of occurrence is unfair since the long IRTs do not have as many chances to occur as the short IRTs. In fact, every time a short IRT occurs, a long IRT cannot; a long IRT has an opportunity to occur only if a shorter IRT does not occur first. Thus, the frequency of the long IRTs should be evaluated only in terms of the occasions on which they could have occurred. In other words, their frequency should be evaluated in terms of the occasions on which the organism waited at least that long — and not also in terms of the short IRTs, when the organism did not wait long enough for long IRTs to have occurred.

This inequity can be taken care of by dealing with the number of IRTs of a given duration per opportunity for their emission. The statistic IRTs/op answers the question: Given that the organism has paused this long since its previous response, what are the chances that it will respond now as opposed to waiting to respond later? It is computed for the IRTs of any given length by dividing the number of IRTs of that length by the total number of IRTs of that length and of greater length, which represents the number of opportunities on which an IRT of that length could occur. The long IRTs are thus not penalized for having had fewer opportunities to occur.

Consider the following example. Suppose that ten IRTs are measured. (In practice, several hundred IRTs are needed before firm conclusions can be drawn from their frequency distribution.) Two

Figure 7.3 A frequency distribution of interresponse times describing the performance on a 10-second drl schedule.

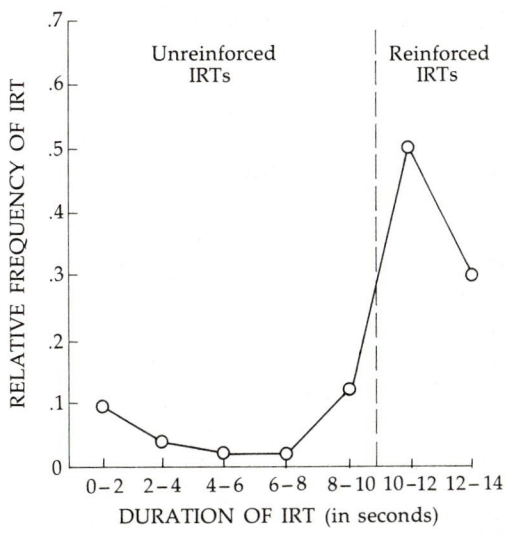

IRTs of each class interval of length are found, as listed in the chart below. These might, for example, be the times between drinking successive glasses of water by a person over about a fifty-hour period.

IRT duration in class intervals of 2 hours	Frequency	Relative frequency	Sum of frequencies	IRTs/op
0–2	2	1/5	10	1/5 (.20)
2–4	2	1/5	8	1/4 (.25)
4–6	2	1/5	6	1/3 (.33)
6–8	2	1/5	4	1/2 (.50)
8–10	2	1/5	2	1/1 (1.00)

In the chart, both the frequency and relative frequency of occurrence indicate that IRTs are equally likely in each class interval. This is perfectly true in the sense that there are equal numbers of each. However, if the drinker has waited until between 4 and 6 hours since the last drink of water, the chances are 2 out of 6, or 1/3, that he will drink between 4 and 6 hours rather than wait and drink later. This fact is shown in the IRTs/op column. In this sense, the probability of a response that terminates the IRT increases the longer the time since the previous response. The longer he waits, the greater the chances he will drink, even though he waits each duration equally often.

When this consideration of frequency per opportunity is applied to the drl performance, the control of the behavior by the time since the previous response is even more striking. What was already a sharply increasing function of time since the last response in terms of the simple frequencies becomes an even steeper function in terms of IRTs/op.

Acquisition of Performance on drl Schedules

The acquisition of the performance on a drl schedule is marked by oscillations in rate. At first, since IRTs long enough for reinforcement do not initially occur, extinction begins and the rate of responding decreases. Then, as the rate decreases, an IRT long enough for reinforcement occurs and is reinforced. Reinforcement, in turn, reinstates a higher rate, and the sequence repeats. No matter how long the required IRT, it will eventually occur during extinction as the rate approaches zero. This safety factor, prohibiting complete extinction, is built in by the schedule. Gradually, the differential reinforcement of IRTs brings responding under the control of the temporal stimuli present when a response is reinforced, and the typical performance illustrated in Figure 7.3 develops.

One reason for the interest in the drl is that it places in opposition two functions of reinforcement: the reinforcement of responses tends to increase the rate of responding, but reinforcement of responses in the presence of the stimuli associated with long IRTs tends to decrease the rate. The stable drl performance seems to be the result of an equilibrium between these two effects.

CONCURRENT SCHEDULES OF REINFORCEMENT

Concurrent scheduling involves reinforcement of two or more responses according to two or more schedules at the same time. In an experimental situation, one schedule may reinforce a pigeon's pecks on the left of two keys while the second schedule reinforces pecks on the right. The schedules are independent of each other and each is independent of the behavior being reinforced according to the other schedule.

Concurrent scheduling is ubiquitous. Even when only one response is reinforced, there is concurrent scheduling in the sense that all other behavior is undergoing extinction. The name *concurrent* is reserved, however, for cases in which an additional explicit schedule is programed in relation to a second response.

Although the individual concurrent schedules are theoretically independent, contingencies resulting from the temporal and spatial association of responses and schedules can result in interactions. One type of interaction may occur, for example, when the responding of a pigeon happens to be reinforced immediately after the bird switches from one response to the other. When this happens, the entire sequence — responding on the first key and switching from the first to the second key — may be reinforced on the schedule associated with the second key. This sequence of responses becomes a chain of behavior which is maintained by the reinforcement delivered after the final peck on the second key. When a chain of this kind develops, responding on the first key may increase to a rate higher than its ordinary level. Although reinforcement may not be currently available on the first key, the bird will frequently switch to it and then switch back to the second key for reinforcement.

A procedure is often added to concurrent schedules in order to suppress this chaining. The procedure requires that a certain period of time must elapse before a response can be reinforced after each switch between keys. A period as short as a half second is sometimes sufficient with pigeons. This procedure helps to ensure that the behavior of switching will never be immediately reinforced. Only the last of a series of pecks on one key is reinforced, never the first response after the switch from one key to the other. The result is an increased independence of the performances on the two schedules.

Other interactions also result from the juxtaposition of the requirements of the component schedules. Although the effects of these interactions do not grossly affect the performances of the component schedules, they are interesting. In the following discussion of the performances typical on four concurrent schedules, we will note these interactions. In each case, we will consider pigeons as subjects and pecking on two different keys as responses.

Concurrent FI and FR Schedules

In concurrent FI and FR schedules, a fixed-interval schedule reinforces responses on one key and a fixed-ratio schedule reinforces responses on the other key. The result is a performance on each key which is relatively independent of the performance on the other key. The performance usually proceeds as follows: After reinforcement on the FI, a few ratios are fulfilled on the other key. These responses are at the high rate typical of FR responding. Then, as the time for reinforcement on the interval approaches, the bird goes to that key and responds in a fashion appropriate to an FI schedule. The FI performances under these conditions generally contain fewer responses than they normally do in isolation, but they still retain the normal FI scallop. The FR performances, when they occur, also retain their typical characteristics. FR responding, however, is almost entirely confined to periods early in the fixed intervals, when FI responding is very infrequent. FR responding may also delay the beginning of responding on the FI schedule slightly beyond the point at which it would ordinarily begin. Thus, when FI and FR schedules are concurrently operating, the bird meshes the two performances, fitting in the FR responding at times when FI reinforcement is not available.

Concurrent VI and (Multiple VI-Extinction) Schedules

In this program, responding on one key is always reinforced on a simple variable-interval schedule. Responding on the other key is reinforced on a multiple schedule: during presentations of one color of light behind the key responding is reinforced on a VI schedule; during presentations of another color, responding is extinguished.

The multiple schedule gains the standard control over pecking on its key. The bird discriminates between the two colors, responding at a low rate during presentations of the stimulus associated with extinction and at a high rate during the stimulus associated with VI reinforcement. The high rate, which replaces the usual moderate rate of responding on the VI schedule, is due to behavioral contrast (as discussed in Chapter 4). The residual responding during extinction can be traced to the level of generalization between the two colors (also discussed in Chapter 4).

Despite the alternately high and low rates of responding on the key maintained by the multiple schedule, the overall rate of responding on the other key maintained by the VI schedule is surprisingly constant. When the extinction component of the multiple schedule is operating, the bird spends most of its time pecking on the other (VI-scheduled) key. Pecking on the simple VI schedule is maintained at the moderate rate appropriate to the VI schedule when used alone.

When the VI component of the multiple schedule is operating, less time is spent responding on the simple VI schedule. When responses on the simple schedule do occur, however, they are emitted at a higher rate than that typical of the ordinary simple VI performance. This higher rate compensates for time spent responding on the other key; it keeps the overall number of VI responses at the same level as when responding occurred only on the simple schedule.

Thus, during the time when reinforcement is available on the multiple schedule, the bird is very busy. It keeps up a high rate of responding on the VI component of the multiple schedule, and it switches frequently to the simple VI-scheduled key where it also responds at a rate high enough to keep the overall rate on that key at an appropriate level. Since the bird cannot peck both keys at once, each performance is disrupted slightly by pauses which occur while the bird is pecking on the other key. But, aside from this necessary irregularity, the performances on both the simple schedule and the multiple schedule retain their identities to a remarkable degree. The bird's maintenance of the typical VI rate on the simple-scheduled key is striking. It prevails despite changes in conditions on the concurrent multiple schedule and despite the high level of activity necessary when reinforcement is available on both keys. At the same time, the bird maintains the discrimination appropriate to the multiple schedule while it is engaged in VI responding. The overall performance on these concurrent schedules testifies to the strength of the control which each of the concurrent components gains over the organism's behavior.

Concurrent VI Schedules

In concurrent VI schedules, an independent variable-interval schedule reinforces responding on each key. The sequence of values of the two VIs may be the same or different, but the two schedules operate independently.

When reinforced on concurrent VI schedules, the pigeon matches the relative frequency of its pecks on each key to the relative frequency of reinforcement obtained on that key. When the VIs are the same, equal numbers of pecks occur on each key. When the VIs are different, the number of pecks on each key will be proportional to the number of reinforcements received on that key. If twenty reinforcements per hour occur as the result of pecks on the left key and forty on the right key, the right key will be pecked twice as frequently as the left. Two thirds of all the pecks in the session will be made on the right key and only one third on the left key. Pigeons are extraordinarily exact in maintaining this relationship, even when three keys are used. Larger numbers of operants have not as yet been systematically investigated.

Concurrent Scheduling of Response Chains

Concurrent scheduling of response chains is an extremely useful procedure in which conditioned reinforcement is substituted for the usual primary reinforcement in concurrent VI schedules. When reinforcement is made available on a key by the VI schedule, the next response, instead of producing food, produces a presentation of a conditioned reinforcer. During the conditioned reinforcer, further responses are reinforced with food. In effect, then, a sequence of two chained schedules is programed on each of two keys. The initial links of the chains are concurrently programed and are independent VI schedules of the same average value. The second, final links consist of other schedules of reinforcement, which are presented separately on each of the keys at the appropriate time. At first, both keys are illuminated and the separate, independent VI schedules go into effect at the same time. When reinforcement becomes available on either of the keys, the next peck on that key is reinforced with the second, final link of that chain. The color of the pecked key changes to indicate the start of the final link, and the other key becomes dark. This second color of the key lasts for a specified, constant period of time, during which further responses on the lighted key are reinforced with food according to the second schedule of reinforcement in that chain. In this way, the second color of each key becomes a discriminative stimulus for the second schedule of reinforcement and a conditioned reinforcer for the first, VI schedule on that key. At the end of the conditioned reinforcer on either key, both keys are lighted with their original colors and the VI schedules go into effect again.

Responding on each key is thus reinforced with presentations of a conditioned reinforcer. The schedules prevailing in the initial concurrent links of the chain are exactly the same. Any differences that develop between left- and right-key responding in the initial links can thus be attributed to differences in the conditioned reinforcers. This is one reason that the schedule is so useful.

Essentially, the procedure provides a scale on which a number of conditions can be weighed and compared. For example, suppose the frequency of reinforcement during the conditioned reinforcers, the final links in the chain, were manipulated. It turns out that the relative frequency of pecking on each key during the concurrent initial links depends on the relative frequency of reinforcement obtained during presentations of the conditioned reinforcers.

A number of other conditions may be compared. In each case, one set of conditions is programed during one conditioned reinforcer, another set of conditions during the other conditioned reinforcer, and the relative frequencies of responding on the two keys during the concurrent initial links of the chain are taken to indicate the relation between the two sets of conditions. The conditioned reinforcing potency of a drl schedule as opposed to a VI schedule may be studied, for example. The effect on the conditioned reinforcer of adding various degrees of punishment can also be assessed.

There are two main advantages to this method. One is that the measured behavior in the initial links is not directly affected by the conditions that are varied in the final links of the chains. For example, when a drl schedule is studied, explicit IRT reinforcement occurs only in the final link of the chain, during the conditioned reinforcer, not in the measured initial link. The other advantage is sensitivity. Changes in the relative frequency of responding in the initial link may occur before any changes are seen in the behavior during the final link. The procedure may be advantageously expanded to include a third key, thus enabling the measurement of three points on a function simultaneously.

As research on more and more complex schedules progresses, we can anticipate results and analyses of increasingly closer applicability to natural situations. It is anyone's guess whether additional basic principles will emerge or whether already known principles will be adequate to explain the results of even the most complex arrangements of reinforcement. In any event, the search is bound to be intriguing.

Up to now, we have discussed schedules of positive reinforcement. Our next concern is with schedules of aversive stimuli and, therefore, with escape, avoidance, and punishment. First, however, we will examine respondent conditioning in more detail.

eight

Respondent behavior and respondent conditioning

Although this is a primer of operant conditioning, in this chapter we will pause for a brief look at respondent behavior and conditioning. Several of the topics in this book—namely, conditioned reinforcement, aversive stimuli, and emotion—intimately involve respondent conditioning. Respondent conditioning is also of historical interest, since present-day research in operant conditioning has grown, at least partially, out of a tradition which began with the study of respondent behavior. For this reason, the conditioning of respondents is sometimes called *classical conditioning*.

In Chapter 1, we saw that respondent behavior is innate—it is part of the inherited structure and function of the organism—and that it is instinctive—its form and occurrence are relatively independent of the organism's experiences with its environment. In order for respondent behavior to occur, however, it must be preceded and elicited by special environmental stimuli. These stimuli are called *unconditioned stimuli* by psychologists. Related stimuli, not so reliably effective in eliciting respondents as classical unconditioned stimuli, have been called *releasers* by naturalists. In the technical vocabulary of operant conditioning, unconditioned stimuli and releasers are called *eliciting stimuli*. Respondent behavior is *elicited* by a prior stimulus, while operant behavior is *emitted* without any apparent prior stimulus. This is one of the most basic distinctions between respondent and operant behavior.

UNCONDITIONED RESPONDENTS

Given the same eliciting stimuli, unconditioned respondents are virtually the same for all biologically equivalent organisms. For example, a light of a given intensity will elicit the same constriction of the pupil in all organisms with the same eye structure. The *latency* of the response—the amount of time that elapses between the presentation of the stimulus and the onset of the response—will be about the same in each case. Latencies of respondents are usually short, so that it is readily apparent that the stimulus produced the response. Nor will other properties of the response, such as the degree and speed of pupil constriction, vary appreciably.

Since the elicitation of unconditioned respondents is so reliable, the rate at which these respondents occur is easy to predict. Although in operant conditioning the influence of environmental variables on the rate of emission of the operant is the most important relationship studied, this is not true for respondents, since their rate of elicitation depends directly on the rate at which the eliciting stimulus is presented.

Habituation of Respondents

Respondents are subject to *habituation,* a gradual decline in the magnitude of the respondent over the course of repeated elicitations. For example, a novice hunter may at first be startled by the loud report of a rifle. As more and more shots are fired, however, the magnitude of the startle decreases. Experienced hunters startle hardly at all. Respondents differ in the degree to which they are subject to habituation. Some, like the constriction of the pupil in bright light, habituate hardly at all, even when they are elicited many times. Others, such as the startle to noise, may habituate so completely that eventually no measurable response is elicited. However, unless it is carried out many times, habituation is normally only temporary. After a period of rest, during which the respondent is not elicited, the magnitude of a habituated respondent usually returns to its normal level.

CONDITIONED RESPONDENTS

Through respondent conditioning, a stimulus that formerly had no effect on a particular respondent acquires the power to elicit that respondent. A stimulus that is not able to elicit a respondent is called a *neutral stimulus* with respect to that respondent. After the stimulus has come to elicit the respondent, it is called a *conditioned stimulus.*

Respondent conditioning does not involve modifying the rate at which the response occurs, as does operant conditioning. Nor does it involve learning new behavior, as does the shaping of operant conditioning. Rather, it involves the taking on by a neutral stimulus of the power to elicit a respondent.

The Respondent Conditioning Procedure

The basic procedure for bringing about respondent conditioning involves repeated presentations of an unconditioned stimulus in a fixed and regular temporal arrangement with the stimulus to be conditioned. The unconditioned stimulus is abbreviated as US, while the conditioned stimulus is abbreviated as CS. Thus, the respondent conditioning procedure arranges for the presentation of the CS together with the US. After a sufficient number of presentations of the two stimuli, the CS, when presented alone, will elicit the respondent formerly elicited only by the US.

In operant conditioning, a response is followed by a (reinforcing) stimulus; in respondent conditioning, the presentation of a stimulus (CS) is followed by the presentation of another stimulus (US). In operant conditioning, the reinforcing stimulus does not occur unless the response occurs. In respondent conditioning, the CS and the US occur in their regular sequence regardless of what the organism is doing.

Five Specific Procedures

The exact temporal relationship between the CS and the US varies from procedure to procedure in respondent conditioning. Traditionally, the relationship remains constant within each individual procedure, but variable intervals between the CS and the US are a potential area for research. Respondent conditioning can be subdivided into five distinct procedures, each of which involves a different temporal relationship between the CS and the US.

Simultaneous conditioning. In the procedure called *simultaneous conditioning,* the CS is first presented continuously. Then, within five seconds of the onset of the CS, the US is presented. Finally, both stimuli terminate together. For example, a ticking metronome (the CS) is turned on, and after three seconds a bit of food (the US) is put into the mouth of the organism. The US, food in the mouth, elicits salivation. After several trials, or presentations of the CS and the US together, conditioning has taken place: the ticking metronome, when presented alone, will also elicit salivation.

Responses elicited by aversive stimuli may also be conditioned in this fashion. Electric shock delivered to the limb of an animal elicits flexion of the limb. If a metronome is started and three seconds later is accompanied by an electric shock, the metronome will become, after a few trials, a CS which elicits the flexion formerly elicited only by the US. In order for this procedure to be respondent conditioning, the electric shock must be unavoidable. If flexion succeeds in avoiding or terminating the shock, the result will be influenced by the different rules governing avoidance conditioning, to be discussed in Chapter 9.

Delayed conditioning. By convention, any procedure in which the CS is presented for more than five seconds before the start of the US is called *delayed conditioning.* In this procedure, the two stimuli still overlap in time, and they still terminate together. After conditioning, the CS elicits the response at about the time when the US used to occur during conditioning.

Trace conditioning. In *trace conditioning*, the CS is presented for a short period of time and then is turned off. After a pause, the US is presented. After trace conditioning, the conditioned response will not follow the CS immediately but will occur at about the same time after the end of the CS as the US did during conditioning.

Backward conditioning. In *backward conditioning,* the CS is presented *after* the US. Backward conditioning is not very effective, if at all.

Temporal conditioning. In *temporal conditioning*, there is no exteroceptive CS. Rather, the US is presented at regular temporal intervals, and the passage of time since the last US becomes the CS. If the US is not presented according to schedule, the conditioned response will be elicited by the temporal stimulus with which the US had previously been presented. The conditioned response usually occurs slightly before the time when the US is due.

Sensitization

In each of these five procedures, it is necessary to watch for a phenomenon called *sensitization*, which may mimic true conditioning. Sometimes a large number of presentations of a US sensitizes the organism so that it will repeat that same response upon the presentation of any new stimulus. For example, after a number of shocks have been delivered to the hind leg of a dog *without* any associated CS, any new stimulus, such as the sound of a buzzer, might elicit flexion of the leg.

Sensitization is a separate phenomenon from conditioning. In conditioning, the CS elicits the response *only* after it has been repeatedly presented with the US. In actual experiments with respondent conditioning, the US alone may be presented to one group of organisms the same number of times that the US is presented with the CS to the group of organisms being conditioned. After these exposures, if the CS elicits the response in the control group, sensitization has occurred and must be taken into account when considering the results of the conditioning procedure. We must always be certain that presentations of the US alone are not sufficient to make the organism mimic true conditioning.

Acquisition in Respondent Conditioning

In contrast to operant conditioning, respondent conditioning proceeds gradually; the power of the new stimulus to elicit the respondent increases slowly during the conditioning process. This is not true in the acquisition of operant behavior, where one effective reinforcement is sufficient to produce a noticeable increase in the frequency of the reinforced response. The temporal course of respondent conditioning is more analogous to the gradual formation of an operant discrimination than it is to operant conditioning.

As a result of respondent conditioning, functions of the US other than the elicitation of gross responses like salivation and flexion are taken over by the CS. Aversive USs, for example, elicit a constellation of responses referred to as *fear*, suppress the rate of positively reinforced behavior, and often increase the rate of negatively reinforced behavior. All these functions may be taken over by the CS as a result of respondent conditioning. Similarly, the parallel but opposite functions of positively reinforcing USs are taken over by CSs. These effects are part of the field of emotion, which will be discussed in Chapter 10.

It is not correct to think of respondent conditioning as simply the substitution of one stimulus, the CS, for another, the US. The conditioned response that the CS comes to elicit is not exactly the same as the unconditioned response elicited by the US. The two responses usually differ slightly in topography, latency, and reliability of elicitation by the stimulus. These differences are minor, however, compared with the many functions of the US that are acquired by the CS.

Extinction of Conditioned Respondents

Extinction of conditioned respondent behavior occurs when the CS is presented without the US a number of times. The magnitude of the response elicited by the CS and the percentage of presentations of the CS which elicit responses gradually become less and less as the

CS continues to be presented without the US. Extinction in respondent conditioning is not the same as in operant conditioning. In the extinction of operant behavior, the response must occur and not be reinforced. In the extinction of respondent behavior, the CS must be presented a number of times without the US. Only occasional presentations of the US, however, seem to be sufficient for the continued effectiveness of the CS.

Spontaneous Recovery

Spontaneous recovery, which occurs during the extinction of operants, also occurs during the extinction of respondents after periods during which neither the US nor the CS is presented. In fact, spontaneous recovery was first studied experimentally during the extinction of a conditioned respondent. If daily sessions are used during extinction, the magnitude of the response elicited by the CS and the percentage of presentations of the CS that elicit the response will both be larger at the beginning of each session than they were at the end of the previous session. The same sort of account of spontaneous recovery during operant extinction as was given in Chapter 3 may also be applied to the spontaneous recovery of respondents.

Disinhibition

The behavior developed during trace and temporal conditioning is particularly subject to a phenomenon called *disinhibition.* The term comes from the assumption that during periods of nonresponding, some active force, inhibition, prevents responses from occurring. This notion has been used to account for the fact that the presentation of a third stimulus — neither the CS nor the US — during extinction tends to increase the effectiveness of the CS. This third, new stimulus is said to *disinhibit* responding. Also, in the trace conditioning procedure, if a novel stimulus is presented to the organism during the period between the onset of the CS and the time when the US usually occurs, responses may occur earlier than usual. Similarly, in the temporal conditioning procedure, when novel stimuli are introduced, premature responses are especially likely to occur between successive presentations of the US. In contrast, the effect of novel stimuli on operant behavior is usually, although not always, to decrease the rate of responding.

Some Respondent Analogues of Operant Conditioning

Although respondent and operant conditioning are two very distinct processes, some analogies can be drawn between the two. A

list of some aspects of respondent conditioning which have counter-
parts in operant conditioning follows.

Generalization

Generalization occurs in respondent, as well as in operant,
conditioning. The power to elicit a respondent, which is developed
by one CS during conditioning, generalizes to other stimuli. The
power of various stimuli to elicit the conditioned respondent is less
the greater the difference between the stimulus and the CS. The
increase in the ability of various stimuli to elicit respondents as
the properties of the stimuli come nearer to those of the CS follows the
same sort of gradient of generalization described in Chapter 4.

Second-Order Conditioning

The respondent analogue of a chain of operant behavior is
second-order conditioning. In this procedure, a well-developed CS is
used, as if it were a US, to impart to a third, neutral stimulus the
power to elicit the respondent. It is not known how far this process
can be carried out, but CSs two or three steps removed from the
original US are not uncommon. As with the primary reinforcer at the
end of a chain, the original US needs to be presented occasionally
with the appropriate, first CS.

Intermittent Presentations of the US

The question naturally arises as to whether there is any analogue
in respondent conditioning of the scheduling of reinforcement in
operant conditioning. Scheduling of reinforcement is not possible
with respondents, since they are elicited rather than emitted. However, it is possible to omit the presentation of the US on some presentations of the CS during conditioning. If this were done in a
systematic fashion, such as presenting the US with the CS only on
every tenth presentation of the CS, it might produce an effect that
would recall some of the effects of schedules of reinforcement. However, the available data suggest that the effectiveness of a CS dimin-
ishes rapidly with increases in the intermittency of its pairing with a
US. Investigation of this area is clearly crucial to a full understanding
of respondent conditioning.

Simultaneous Operant and Respondent Conditioning

Whenever the US in the respondent conditioning procedure is a
positive or negative reinforcer, operant conditioning occurs at the

same time as respondent conditioning. Similarly, whenever the reinforcer in the operant procedure is a US, respondent conditioning proceeds at the same time as operant conditioning. Thus, insofar as the classes of stimuli — eliciting stimuli and reinforcing stimuli — are composed of the same stimuli, operant and respondent conditioning are coextensive.

Consider a case of respondent conditioning in which the presentation of the US is a positive reinforcer. Despite the fact that no behavior (either operant or respondent) is required to cause the US to appear, the presentation of the US will nevertheless reinforce any operant that happens to precede it. A superstitious response may be built up (as discussed in Chapter 3). Also, the CS becomes a conditioned reinforcer, which may then superstitiously reinforce behavior that happens to precede its presentation. In the case where the US is a negative reinforcer, any operant that happens to occur just before the withdrawal of the US will be reinforced, despite the fact that no response actually causes the withdrawal. Again, superstitious behavior may be created.

If the positive or negative reinforcer in an operant conditioning procedure is also a US, the procedure arranges that the other stimuli prevailing at the moment of reinforcement will be repeatedly paired with the US. Thus, respondent conditioning will take place. The respondents elicited by the reinforcer (US) will also come to be elicited by the stimuli prevailing at the moment of reinforcement (CS). For example, in the fixed-interval schedule, the reinforcer occurs at relatively regular time intervals. If the reinforcer is a US, this will be the same as the temporal conditioning of respondents, and the same effect will be obtained. Salivation, originally elicited by the reinforcing food in the mouth, will come to be elicited by the temporal stimuli present at the time of reinforcement. The result of the fixed-interval schedule on the operant behavior of the organism will be the scalloped rate of responding. Its effect on the respondent behavior of the organism will be to condition the temporal stimuli, which will then elicit salivation as the time at which reinforcement has previously appeared approaches.

The procedure arranges for both operant and respondent conditioning, but the two remain independent of each other. There is no reason to think of the salivation as causing the operant behavior or of the operant behavior as causing the salivation. This distinction is often muddled in cases where the reinforcer is the withdrawal of an aversive stimulus. The withdrawal of the aversive stimulus increases the rate of the preceding operant behavior. At the same time, the respondents elicited by the aversive stimulus are conditioned to the prevailing stimuli. One very often hears that the conditioned respondents, which usually go under the names of fear and anxiety, *cause* the avoidance behavior. The contention is that the aversive character of the situation elicits the anxiety and that the anxiety then brings about the avoidance. While it is true that the anxiety is elicited, the avoidance behavior may, in fact, be an independent, conditioned operant. Neither one causes the other; rather, both are products of the same procedure which arranges for simultaneous operant and respondent conditioning.

nine

Aversive control: escape, avoidance, and punishment

So far in discussing the influence of the environment on operant behavior, we have confined ourselves almost entirely to positive reinforcing stimuli, whose *presentation* increases the probability of a response. In this chapter, we shall discuss the influence of stimuli whose *withdrawal* increases the rate of responding: the aversive stimuli. The process of maintaining behavior by withdrawing aversive stimuli is called *negative reinforcement.* When the withdrawal of an aversive stimulus maintains or increases the rate of responding, the stimulus is called a *negative reinforcer.*

Two paradigms in which aversive stimuli increase or maintain responding are escape and avoidance. In *escape,* a response terminates an aversive stimulus *after* the stimulus has begun; the organism cannot avoid the beginning of the aversive stimulus. In *avoidance,* a response avoids or postpones the beginning of the aversive stimulus. Escape and avoidance sometimes occur in combination. Thus, between presentations of the aversive stimulus, responses postpone its start; once it has started, responses terminate it.

A paradigm called *punishment* is often used in an attempt to reduce the rate of responding. In punishment, responses are followed by an aversive stimulus.

The experimental apparatus used to study the effects of aversive stimuli on operant behavior is essentially the same as the apparatus described in Chapter 2. Instead of, or as well as, a means of delivering positive reinforcement, the apparatus includes a means of delivering the aversive stimulus — usually electric shock delivered to the animal's feet through metal bars forming the floor of the experimental chamber. With this method, however, the amount of shock received may vary as the animal jumps or runs around the chamber in response to the shock. Also, since the animal's jumping and running do in fact reduce the shock, there may be some interference with the response being measured in the experiment. A more reliable method of delivering shock is through electrodes implanted in the body of the animal—for example, under a fold of skin on a rat's back. If the electrodes are secure, the animal's movements will have no influence on the intensity or duration of the shock it receives.

ESCAPE

Acquisition of Escape

We have seen that escape involves responses that terminate an aversive stimulus after it has begun. In the acquisition of escape, when an aversive stimulus is first presented to an organism, it usually elicits some respondents, such as running and jumping around the chamber. These respondents, together with the natural and learned operant behavior of the organism, eventually result in the performance of the desired response, which is then reinforced by the termination of the aversive stimulus. Thus, a rat may fall upon the lever in the chamber as he jumps around in response to the shock, or he may approach and press the bar because of previous experience. It seems to make little difference whether the reinforced response is initially respondent or operant in origin. Once the behavior is reinforced by termination of the shock, it will tend to occur earlier on subsequent presentations of the aversive stimulus. It is reinforced as an operant response, regardless of its origins.

After the first few reinforcements, there is usually a high probability that the organism will emit the response even when the aversive stimulus is not present. This happens for two reasons. First, the response has been reinforced and thus has a substantial tendency to reoccur. Second, all the discriminative stimuli (except for the aversive stimulus) which were present at the time of reinforcement are also present after the termination of the aversive stimulus, and they result in the generalization of the response to times when the aversive stimulus is not present. Gradually, however, during subsequent presentations of the aversive stimulus, a discrimination is perfected between the presence and absence of the aversive stimulus. The response that terminates the aversive stimulus comes to occur almost entirely in its presence because only then is it reinforced. There is a residual level of responding when the aversive stimulus is not present, as there is in nearly all discriminations; but it is very low. Thus, in escape, the aversive stimulus itself is the discriminative stimulus in the presence of which the response is reinforced by the termination of the aversive stimulus.

Maintenance of Escape

Escape is maintained in the same fashion as other operant behavior. We might arrange, for example, that the tenth response will shut off the shock, thus programing a fixed-ratio schedule of escape. Schedules of reinforcement seem to maintain the same patterns of behavior when the withdrawal of an aversive stimulus is the reinforcer as they do when the presentation of food is the reinforcer.

The rate of responding maintained by escape is a function of the intensity of the aversive stimulus, just as the rate of responding maintained by food is a function of the degree of deprivation. As the intensity of the aversive stimulus increases, the rate of responding increases, as it does with greater deprivation. In both cases, however, extremely intense motivational conditions are disadvantageous; the extremes of deprivation and of intensity produce insufficient responding and perhaps a dead organism.

A curious phenomenon often occurs in studies of the intensity of the aversive stimulus. After the training and maintenance of escape with aversive stimuli of varying intensities, the withdrawal of extremely low intensities of the aversive stimulus may be sufficient to maintain responding. These intensities may be well below those that were completely ineffective in reinforcing escape before training, and they may also elicit no visible respondents. Nevertheless, they are aversive, since their withdrawal is reinforcing. This is one reason for the functional definition of an aversive stimulus as a stimulus whose withdrawal reinforces responding. A definition in terms of elicited respondents would not account for the behavior maintained by aversive stimuli of such low intensity.

Sometimes in experiments with aversive stimuli, another, competing response accidentally becomes available to the animal. For example, since the aversive stimulus does not occur outside of the experimental chamber, the animal may initially engage in responses that would get it out of the chamber, if that were possible. These responses compete and interfere with the response under study in the experiment. If the chamber is made secure, these responses disappear and the organism eventually engages in the one response that does, in fact, result in escape from the aversive stimulus.

Also, the respondent behavior elicited by the aversive stimulus — such as the running and jumping we have already noted — may interfere with performance of the operant. As acquisition proceeds, however, these respondents usually habituate, so that their interference with the operant under study is minimal.

Care must be taken in the design of the experimental apparatus to see that no competing responses are unintentionally reinforced. We have already noted that when shock is delivered through a metal grid floor, responses such as running and jumping may actually decrease the shock. Thus, the animal may emit fewer of the more effective responses than it would if they were the only responses reinforced. We have seen that this sort of alternative response can be eliminated by delivering the shock through implanted electrodes.

Extinction of Escape

Extinction of escape can be carried out in either of two ways. In one procedure, the aversive stimulus is presented but occurrences of the response are no longer reinforced by the termination of the aversive stimulus. This procedure results in a slow, usually erratic decrease in the frequency of the response.

In the second method of extinguishing escape, the aversive stimulus is no longer presented. This method, in addition to no longer reinforcing responding, also eliminates one of the discriminative stimuli (the aversive stimulus) formerly associated with reinforcement. Because other stimuli that were present when the response was reinforced are still present during extinction, some responses do occur during extinction with this procedure, as they do between shocks during maintenance. Extinction is rapid, however. The lack of one of the discriminative stimuli controlling the response (the aversive stimulus) and the already low tendency to emit the response in the absence of the aversive stimulus combine with the lack of reinforcement to produce rapid extinction. This procedure is actually more analogous to greatly decreased deprivation than to extinction in the case of positive reinforcement.

AVOIDANCE

An avoidance procedure allows the organism to postpone or, theoretically at least, to avoid completely the aversive stimulus. Avoidance is sometimes instituted after escape has been acquired, but it is more commonly instituted without previous training of the organism. In the acquisition of avoidance, an exteroceptive stimulus, such as light, is presented to the organism, and after a period of time, such as thirty seconds, an aversive stimulus is presented. The two stimuli overlap in time, and they terminate together. If the organism emits the required response during the presentation of the light prior to the aversive stimulus, the aversive stimulus does not occur, the light shuts off, and there is a pause of a specified length before the light is presented again.

Factors Maintaining Avoidance with an Exteroceptive Stimulus

The procedure described above—of following the onset of a neutral stimulus with an unconditioned stimulus—is the same as the procedure used in delayed respondent conditioning (see Chapter 8). Thus, the exteroceptive light becomes a CS which elicits respondents previously elicited only by the unconditioned aversive stimulus.

At the same time that this respondent conditioning takes place, the operant response is also conditioned, since its occurrences are reinforced both by the termination of the conditioned aversive stimulus and by the continued absence of the unconditioned aversive stimulus.

A discrimination is also formed. Initially, there may be substantial responding between presentations of the light. However, as with escape, the discrimination between the conditioned aversive stimulus and the stimuli prevailing between trials is gradually perfected, and the light is established as a discriminative stimulus.

The conditioned aversive stimulus thus comes to have several functions. It elicits the respondents previously elicited only by the unconditioned aversive stimulus. In addition to functioning as a CS, the conditioned aversive stimulus has two operant properties. First, it is a conditioned negative reinforcer, since its withdrawal becomes reinforcing; and, second, it is a discriminative stimulus in the presence of which the response is reinforced both by the termination of itself, the conditioned stimulus, and by the continued absence of the unconditioned stimulus.

In avoidance, then, the conditioned aversive stimulus (here the light) has the same operant functions as did the unconditioned stimulus (the shock) in escape. Thus, in avoidance, the animal not only avoids the unconditioned aversive stimulus but also escapes from the conditioned aversive stimulus.

It is possible to demonstrate directly that the withdrawal of a conditioned aversive stimulus is reinforcing. In fact, this is one of the classical demonstrations in the field of aversive control. First, with no response available, the organism is simply exposed to the light and, in its presence, to the aversive stimulus. That is to say, respondent conditioning is carried out, and the light becomes a CS. Then, the aversive US is no longer presented, and the CS is presented alone. An operant response in the presence of the conditioned aversive stimulus results in its termination. The termination of the CS is sufficient to reinforce the response, and the rate of the response increases. Thus, the respondent CS is also a conditioned negative reinforcer whose withdrawal will reinforce responding.

Although responding in avoidance can be partially accounted for by escape from the conditioned aversive stimulus, the absence of the unconditioned aversive stimulus must also follow if responding is to be maintained efficiently. Even if the response does not immediately terminate the conditioned stimulus, the fact that it results in the absence of the unconditioned aversive stimulus is sufficient to maintain responding.

The temporary absence of an aversive stimulus may seem like a strange reinforcer. Some psychologists, in order to avoid this awkwardness, prefer to speak of the attainment of "safety" rather than the relief from aversiveness as the reinforcer in escape and avoidance. However, the aversive stimulus is, in fact, presented by the environment and subsequently withdrawn after a response; and there is no question that organisms do, in fact, respond to the absence of a stimulus. If one of a regular series of events (electric shocks in this specific case) is omitted, the behavior of the organism immediately reveals that its absence has an effect. For these reasons, operant conditioning has chosen to keep the original terminology and to refer to the absence of the aversive stimulus as a reinforcer in the case of avoidance.

We saw previously that both interval schedules and the drl have an inherent safety factor guarding against extinction: if a response is not emitted for some time, reinforcement will become available during that time so that only one occurrence of the response is necessary for reinforcement. Avoidance also has an inherent safety factor. The conditioned aversive stimulus gradually loses its effectiveness as a negative reinforcer if it is not, at least occasionally, accompanied by the aversive stimulus (the electric shock). Thus, if the organism continually responds in time to avoid the shock, the conditioned aversive stimulus becomes less effective; eventually its withdrawal no longer reinforces responding, and responding begins to extinguish. Then the safety factor comes into operation. Whenever the organism fails to respond in time, the shock occurs and the effectiveness of the conditioned aversive stimulus is reinstated. This gradual waning of the tendency to avoid followed by the reinstatement of adequate avoidance by a shock is a general characteristic of much avoidance.

Extinction of Avoidance Behavior

We have just seen that continued presentations of the conditioned stimulus without the unconditioned stimulus result in a decrease in the effectiveness of the conditioned stimulus, to the point where its withdrawal will no longer reinforce avoidance. Hence, if shock is never presented, avoidance will extinguish for lack of reinforcement.

Also, avoidance will normally extinguish if the unconditioned stimulus, the shock, occurs regardless of whether the animal responds during the conditioned stimulus. These two kinds of extinction are parallel to the two kinds of extinction of escape responding described earlier in this chapter.

Temporal Avoidance Conditioning

It is not necessary for the conditioned aversive stimulus in avoidance conditioning to be exteroceptive. The following procedure, for example, involves the passing of time as a stimulus: essentially, an operant procedure is added to temporal respondent conditioning, just as in the avoidance procedure just described, an operant procedure was added to delayed respondent conditioning.

The aversive stimulus, a very short electric shock, is presented to the organism at regular intervals, say, every ten seconds. Each occurrence of a response, for example a lever-press, postpones the next occurrence of the shock for a period of time; twenty seconds is typical. The period of time between shocks delivered in the absence of responding is called the shock-shock interval, or *SS-interval*. The period of time by which the response postpones the aversive stimulus is called the response-shock interval, or *RS-interval*. Thus, if the SS-interval is ten seconds, the aversive stimulus will occur regularly every ten seconds if there is no responding. If the RS-interval is twenty seconds, each response that occurs programs the next occurrence of the aversive stimulus for twenty seconds later, regardless of how much time has passed since the occurrence of the last aversive stimulus or the last response. If the organism responds again during any twenty-second RS-interval, there is another postponement for twenty seconds. This schedule maintains avoidance well; the aversive stimulus usually occurs infrequently.

A temporal discrimination usually develops, although avoidance can be very good without it. The temporal discrimination is best seen in a distribution of the interresponse times, the IRTs. The frequency with which IRTs occur increases with the duration of the IRT, up to a length near the time when the aversive stimulus is due. This discrimination is maintained with an accuracy and a gradient similar to that maintained by the drl schedule (discussed in Chapter 7), which also generates a temporal discrimination.

If the interval by which a response postpones the next occurrence of the aversive stimulus is increased, the rate of responding decreases and the temporal discrimination described above is adjusted. However, the average rate of responding is always considerably higher than the minimal rate required by the schedule for the complete avoidance of the aversive stimulus. Aversive stimuli do still sometimes occur because the IRTs are variable and an occasional IRT is longer than the RS-interval. Long IRTs are sometimes due to the onset of extinction, which results when the aversive stimulus has been avoided for some time.

When a temporal discrimination is formed, the temporal stimulus associated with the unconditioned aversive stimulus not only becomes a discriminative stimulus but also becomes a respondent CS and a conditioned negative reinforcer. We can call this temporal stimulus "a long time since the last response." This stimulus becomes a conditioned aversive stimulus because it is accompanied by the unconditioned aversive stimulus: when it is "a long time since the last response," the unconditioned aversive stimulus is delivered. After several presentations of the unconditioned aversive stimulus at "a long time since the last response," that time becomes a conditioned aversive stimulus, and, hence, its withdrawal is reinforcing. A response results in its withdrawal, since after a response has occurred, it is no longer "a long time since the last response." Thus, in temporal avoidance conditioning, the temporal stimulus correlated with the arrival of the shock has the same three functions as the exteroceptive stimuli in ordinary avoidance conditioning: it is a discriminative stimulus, in whose presence the organism's avoidance response is reinforced; it is a conditioned aversive stimulus, which reinforces responding by its withdrawal; and it is a CS, which concurrently elicits the respondents elicited by the unconditioned aversive stimulus.

Avoidance and Emotion

Although a treatment of emotion and its relation to reinforcing and eliciting stimuli follows in Chapter 10, we will briefly discuss here the connection between avoidance behavior and emotions such as fear and anxiety.

We often say that we avoid an aversive stimulus because we are afraid of it, or because we dislike it, or because it annoys us. Although this sort of statement is accurate enough for everyday use, it does not really describe the conditions controlling our behavior. What such statements actually describe is not the negative reinforcers that maintain our avoidance behavior but the respondents, mainly emotional, which are concurrently elicited by the conditioned aversive stimuli based on the aversive stimulus we are avoiding. Although these emotions do play a part in avoidance, they are not necessarily the only factors essential for its maintenance. And more important, if we seek to control, modify, or eliminate avoidance behavior, we may make as much headway by altering the environmental determinants of avoidance as by trying to modify the emotions accompanying avoidance. The withdrawal of the conditioned aversive stimulus and reinforcement by the absence of the unconditioned aversive stimulus emerge as effective in the maintenance of avoidance behavior. Emotions may also occur in connection with avoidance, but they are not necessarily its primary causes.

PUNISHMENT

Punishment is the technical term for the presentation of an aversive stimulus following and dependent upon the occurrence of an operant. Punishment may be administered to an operant that has never been reinforced, to an operant that is being maintained by reinforcement, or to an operant that is being extinguished. Punishment may follow responding maintained by positive or negative reinforcement. When studying the effects of punishment on maintained responding, it is, of course, important to specify exactly the maintaining conditions, such as the schedule of reinforcement. Punishment itself may be scheduled: it is not necessary to punish every response any more than it is necessary to reinforce every response. However, the case in which every response is punished has been studied most extensively.

Punishment of Maintained Behavior

The experiment described below punishes every response maintained on a variable-interval schedule of positive reinforcement. The organism is a pigeon, and the aversive stimulus is an electric current passed through two electrodes implanted in the bird's chest. The operant is key pecking.

The average daily performances resulting from this procedure are illustrated in Figure 9.1. No responses are punished during the first five sessions, in order to establish the normal rate of responding on the variable-interval schedule. In the sixth session, each response is punished with a shock of moderate intensity, and the rate of responding on the variable-interval schedule immediately decreases. Over the next few sessions, moderate punishment is continued, but there is a gradual recovery in the pigeon's behavior. The rate of responding slowly increases until it reaches a level that is maintained until punishment is discontinued for a few sessions. When punishment stops, in session 11, the rate of responding increases abruptly, up to a *higher* level than that previously maintained by the schedule of positive reinforcement alone. Over the next few sessions, the rate returns to the level formerly maintained by the variable-interval schedule.

Session 16 begins a period in which each response is punished with a shock of higher intensity. The rate of responding decreases below the level to which it was driven by less intense punishment, but, again, there is some recovery over the next few sessions. When punishment is again discontinued, the rate again shoots up—even higher than when it was first discontinued—and then gradually declines to its former unpunished level.

Beginning with session 26, punishment is the least intense in the experiment. As expected, the rate decreases, but less than previously, and then it recovers. After punishment ceases, the rate rises slightly above its former level and then levels off and returns to the base-line, variable-interval performance.

These results indicate that although punishment suppresses responding, it does not necessarily abolish it. The suppression is greatest when punishment is first introduced; later there is some recovery. The maintained level of responding with punishment is an inverse function of the intensity of the punishment: the rate is lower the more intense the punishment. Also, very intense punishment may completely eliminate responding, whereas very weak punishment may have no effect at all.

When punishment is discontinued, the rate of responding increases up to a level higher than that originally maintained by the schedule (another instance of behavioral contrast). Here we have one of the pitfalls in the use of punishment in the efficient control of behavior: punishment is successful in reducing the tendency to engage in the punished behavior; but to remain effective, punishment must be continued. If the behavior is no longer punished, there is a greater tendency than ever to engage in the behavior. This should not surprise us, since we have seen that the effect of reinforcement is not permanent once reinforcement is discontinued. Unless the punishment is very severe, it is effective only as long as it is continued. The immediate consequences of behavior usually outweigh consequences that prevailed in the distant past.

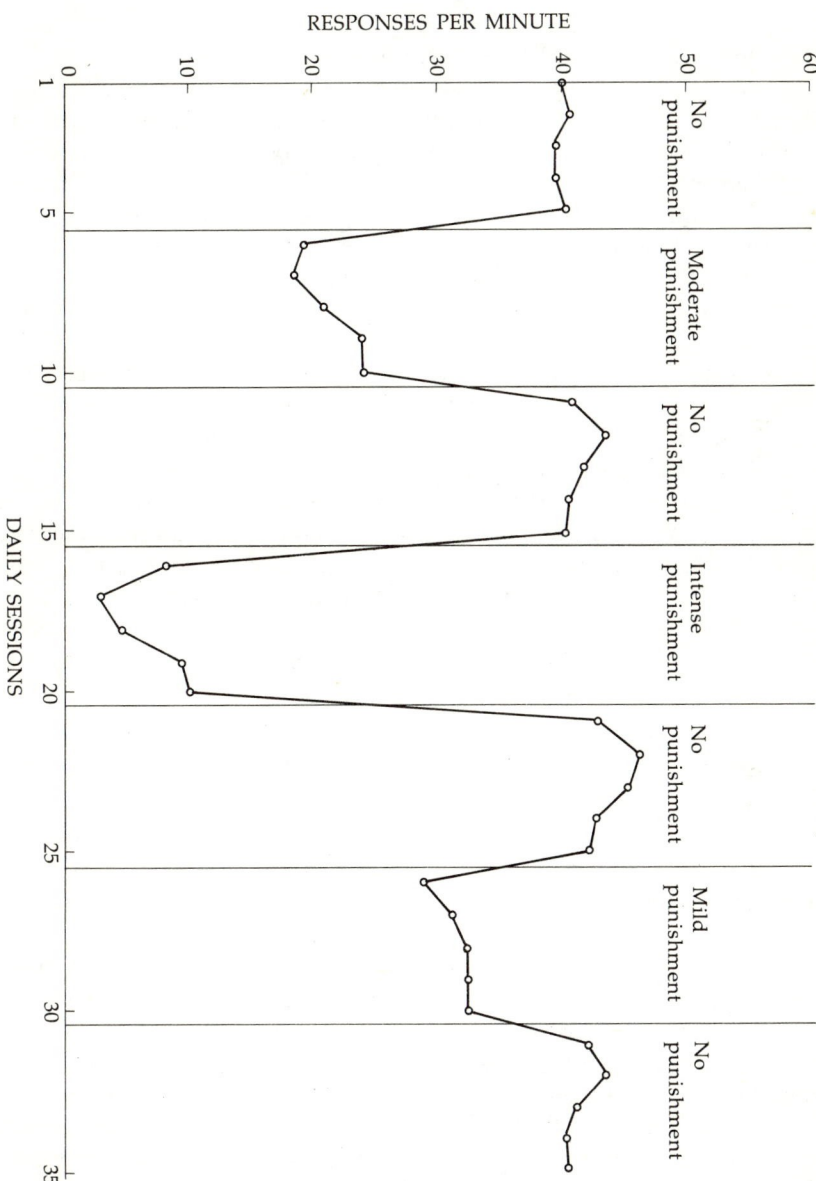

Figure 9.1 Some of the effects of moderate, intense, and mild punishment, each followed by no punishment, on responding maintained by positive reinforcement.

Although these results are applicable to the rate of maintained behavior in an organism having prior experience with punishment, they may not occur when punishment is first administered. When punishment first occurs, respondent behaviors, such as running and jumping around, may appear; or the animal may attempt to get out of the chamber altogether. The respondent behaviors will gradually attenuate, through habituation (see Chapter 8); and as long as the attempts to escape or avoid the punishment are not reinforced — that is, when the chamber is secure and the aversive stimulus is efficiently delivered — these attempts will also eventually cease. While these alternative behaviors persist, however, they can interfere with the precise measurement of the pure effects of punishment by competing with the performance of the punished response. The measured effects of punishment are then contaminated with the additional attempts at escape and avoidance.

In punishment, as in escape and avoidance, it is important to use an aversive stimulus that is completely immune to modification by the behavior of the organism. In addition, it is important to give the animal enough experience with the experimental arrangement so that contaminating respondent and operant behavior will attenuate. Only after these precautions have been taken can the orderly effects shown in Figure 9.1 be expected.

Effects of Punishment on Other Reinforced Behavior

If responding in the presence of one discriminative stimulus is punished and responding in the presence of another is not, responding in the presence of the stimulus associated with punishment will be suppressed while responding in the presence of the other discriminative stimulus will actually increase. Punishment thus indirectly acts to facilitate some behavior.

This effect can be shown by introducing, withdrawing, and reintroducing punishment during one of two variable-interval components of a multiple schedule. (Multiple schedules are discussed in Chapter 7.) The changes in behavior during the punished component of the schedule are similar to those shown in Figure 9.1. When punishment is introduced, the rate of the punished responding decreases and then recovers somewhat. When punishment is discontinued, the punished behavior is facilitated and then levels off. When punishment is reintroduced, the punished behavior again drops off and recovers.

Meanwhile, the unpunished behavior in the other component of the multiple schedule follows an opposite course. When punishment is introduced into the first component, the rate of the unpunished responding increases. When punishment is discontinued, the unpunished responding drops back to its base-line rate. This effect is reminiscent of behavioral contrast, which occurs when responding is extinguished in one component of a multiple schedule and continues to be reinforced in another component. The effect of the extinction in one component is to increase responding in the second component.

These effects also have practical applications. We cannot expect that punishing a certain behavior under one set of conditions will reduce or eliminate that behavior under all conditions. Quite the opposite actually happens: the behavior is facilitated when it is no longer punished. Thus, spanking a child for misbehaving may be beneficial as long as the person who does the spanking is present. But when the spanker leaves or the child goes to school, the punished behavior may actually become more frequent than it was before punishment.

Punishment with Various Schedules of Reinforcement and with Extinction

The effects of punishment also depend, to a large extent, on the schedule of positive reinforcement which maintains the punished responding. Figure 9.1 illustrates the general changes in rate obtained with variable-interval reinforcement. Roughly the same changes can be expected to occur with any schedule of reinforcement, although different schedules cause characteristic modifications in the general pattern. For example, the rate of responding on a fixed-interval schedule is lowered by moderate intensities of punishment, but the typical FI acceleration of responding through the interval is not eliminated. The high and constant rate maintained by a fixed-ratio schedule is not affected by moderate punishment of each response; rather, the pause after reinforcement tends to become longer the more intense the punishment.

When punishment is delivered for a short period of time during extinction following positive reinforcement, the rate of responding further decreases during the period of punishment. However, an increase of the sort examined above follows after the termination of punishment. The result is that the total number of responses during extinction is changed very little by the period of punishment.

Punishment of responding controlled by aversive stimuli presents methodological intricacies. One difficulty is that the punishment should be different from the aversive stimulus whose withdrawal is the reinforcer maintaining the responding. If they are the same, the effects of punishment may be contaminated by some of the functions of the aversive stimulus in the maintenance process. Apparently, the effects of punishment on aversively controlled behavior are substantially the same as those cited above. However, complications arise when the intensity of the punishment approaches the intensity of the aversive stimulus whose withdrawal reinforces the responding.

Punishment as a Discriminative Stimulus

Punishment need not always produce a decrease in the rate of responding. Suppose that the response is punished only on those occasions when it is also reinforced and that the response is not punished when it is not reinforced. In this situation, punishment becomes a discriminative stimulus, as in other multiple schedules, and the rate of responding will be high in the presence of punishment, which is the occasion for reinforcement, and low in the absence of punishment, which is associated with nonreinforcement. When punishment is a discriminative stimulus associated with reinforcement, punished responding occurs at a higher rate than unpunished responding.

In some instances, the presentation of what is, under ordinary circumstances, an aversive stimulus may reinforce behavior. Masochism may be such a case. The procedures that bring about this peculiar state of affairs are not known with any accuracy at present, but the phenomenon has been demonstrated in the laboratory by involving the aversive stimulus in a chain based in part on positive reinforcement. The effect is thus subject to an experimental analysis and, hence, to eventual control and understanding.

ADDITIONAL AVERSIVE CONDITIONS

Most conditions involving aversive stimuli or extinction are in themselves aversive. The fact that extinction is aversive has been demonstrated in the laboratory. Naturally, punishment and escape are aversive, since they involve the presentation of aversive stimuli. The fact that avoidance programs are also aversive has been shown by experiments which provide a response that allows the animal to escape from the avoidance schedule. In these experiments, responding is maintained by the withdrawal of the conditions under which the organism must avoid.

Aversive schedules vary in their degree of aversiveness. The amount of aversiveness seems to depend, at least in part, on the intensity of the aversive stimulus, the frequency with which it is presented, and, in the case of avoidance, on the frequency with which the animal must respond in order to prevent the occurrence of the aversive stimulus.

Two sets of aversive conditions may be pitted against each other, as in the following experiment. One of two stimuli is always present in the chamber, either a tone or a light. During the light, responses postpone the next occurrence of a shock by ten seconds. If a shock occurs, the light terminates and the tone begins. During the tone, responses postpone the light by thirty seconds. If thirty seconds elapse without a response during the tone, the tone ceases and the light begins again.

The outcome is that during the light the organism may take the shock much more frequently than it would if the ten-second schedule were used alone. The animal seems to endure the shock because during the tone less frequent responding is required to avoid the light and hence the eventual shock. Thus, the thirty-second condition prevailing in the presence of the tone, plus the shock required to obtain it, seem to be less aversive than continued responding on the ten-second condition.

The fact that the use of aversive stimuli to control behavior is in itself aversive, plus the fact that the aversive control of one part of the animal's behavior can have far-reaching and sometimes undesirable effects on the rest of its behavior, makes aversive stimuli less practical than positive reinforcers in controlling behavior in natural settings. This is not to say that aversive control is ineffective. Aversive stimuli have a very strong influence on behavior, and often the use of aversive stimuli is the only available means for the control of a given behavior. Yet it is probably true that aversive control is used more widely in our society than is necessary. Such developments as permissive child raising and progressive education show that the undesirable side effects of aversive control have been given some notice, but the relationship between aversive control and its ramifications has been so poorly understood that most remedial attempts have met with little, if any, success. As the experimental analysis of the control of behavior by aversive stimuli progresses, the relations between aversively controlled and other behavior should become clearer. Greater understanding should not only encourage the use of positive reinforcement where possible but also may provide more desirable ways of controlling behavior through aversive stimuli.

ten

Emotion and motivation

WHAT IS AN EMOTION?

An emotion is a complex response elicited and occasioned by environmental conditions and composed of both operants and respondents. Some of the components of emotion are visible and easily accessible to other individuals; these are the so-called "expressive behaviors." Other components are invisible and discriminable only by the organism experiencing the emotion. Operant conditioning emphasizes the fact that invisible emotional responses are only one of several components of emotion.

Respondent and Operant Components of Emotion

Typically, the respondent components of emotion are of two classes, invisible and visible. The invisible respondents are specifiable changes in the internal structure of the organism—for example, the changes associated with butterflies in the stomach and changes in the size of the blood vessels in various parts of the body. If some of the latter are pronounced, blushing may occur, rendering the change visible and easily accessible to other organisms.

Another class of invisible respondents involves the discriminations an organism makes between stimuli that are pleasant and unpleasant. These respondents can be elicited, for example, with aqueous solutions of salt or sugar. As the concentration of these solutions increases from zero, they at first become more pleasant but soon change to unpleasant. The pleasantness or unpleasantness is discriminated as a stimulus by the organism and can be reported. The report, an operant occasioned by the invisible respondent, is one of three major types of operants composing an emotion.

Expressive behavior, such as smiling, crying, and grimacing, is the second class of respondents in an emotion. The expressive behavior is, of course, visible and easily accessible to other organisms.

Expressive behavior may also be operant—it is the second major operant component of emotion. An experimental analysis and a detailed history of the organism are needed in each individual case in order to decide whether a given instance of expressive behavior is respondent or operant. A child's frown, for example, is often—and surely in the first months—a respondent component of sadness; but later it may be an operant, occasioned by situations in which frowning is reinforced. Actors have highly developed operant repertoires of expressive behavior.

Operant expressive behavior closely resembles respondent expressive behavior. It must do so in order to be reinforced by its audience; we are not often moved by bad actors. Since the operant expressive behaviors are present when the respondent components of the emotion are elicited, the operants become conditioned stimuli through ordinary respondent conditioning. Their occurrence as operants may therefore come to elicit the respondent components of the emotion. Thus, the actor may begin by imitating the expressions of sadness and end up being truly sad himself. The operant and respondent components of an emotion are thus closely and functionally interrelated.

The Name of an Emotion

The third and final operant component of an emotion is its name. The sad person responds to his own behavior by naming it sadness, for example. The name of an emotion is an operant emitted in the presence of the other components of the emotion and reinforced by another individual or by an audience. The names of our emotions are operants, which we acquire through experience.

An operant of naming is reinforced only when the situation in which the person appears and the visible behavior of the person are appropriate to the name of the emotion. The response "I'm happy" is not normally reinforced if the person is in a situation which usually provokes fear or if the person frowns. Thus, although the name of an emotion is emitted in the presence of both visible and invisible stimuli, it is reinforced by the audience only if it is appropriate to the visible stimuli. The inaccessible stimuli, mainly furnished by respondents, come to participate in the control of the name of the emotion by accident; they happen to be present when the name is reinforced. The reason that there is any consistency at all in the internal states called by a given name is that people are similarly structured; thus, each situation in which the name is reinforced elicits a similar constellation of respondents from each of the persons naming the emotion.

Some emotions, such as love and joy, seem more diffuse and are more difficult to define than others, such as fear and anger. This is owing not only to the greater variability in the situations which produce love and joy but also to the less well-defined behavior to which audiences respond in the cases of love and joy. It is much easier to reinforce the appropriate use of the name *fear* than the name *love*.

The name of an emotion may come to act as a conditioned stimulus that elicits the respondent components of the emotion. In other words, respondent conditioning may take place, since the name of the emotion, like the operant expressive behavior of the actor, is associated with the environmental unconditioned stimuli that naturally elicit the respondent components of the emotion.

Stimulus Control of the Name of an Emotion

Since the audiences that reinforce the names of emotions rely in part on the environment outside the organism, the names of the emotions come to be responses to the environment as well as to conditions inside the organism. A simple example is the typical response of an acquaintance to the question, "How are you?" The response is usually of the sort, "Fine, thanks," regardless of how the acquaintance actually feels at that moment. The reply is controlled more by the question from the external environment than by the internal environment, or the person's actual feelings. Similarly, the seducer says, "I love you"; the child, "I am afraid"; the wife, "I am happy" — perhaps not at all in response to existing internal conditions but in response to external environmental conditions. Doubtless one of the plagues of the medical profession is the descriptive verbal responses actually under the control of external conditions that are made in answer to questions calling for the description of internal states and feelings. Witness the hypochondriac. The fact that such people may really feel their symptoms is in part a result of the same conditioning process whereby the actor comes to cry from initially only imitating sadness.

THE EXPERIMENTAL STUDY OF EMOTION

Since the naming and describing of emotions depend on both internal and external stimulation, verbal behavior may not be a reliable index of the presence of a particular emotion. To define sadness as the state of persons who say they are sad is potentially misleading. Nor can the feelings themselves — the inaccessible respondent components of the emotion — be studied directly by the psychologist. They are inside the skin of the organism, and this location traditionally places them in the province of physiology. In any event, they are not normally accessible to anyone but the organism experiencing the emotion and cannot therefore be dealt with directly in a scientific and experimental study of behavior.

The alternative adopted by operant conditioning is to study the behavioral effects of environmental circumstances that are thought to produce emotion. These are situations in which a reinforcing community would reinforce the naming of the appropriate emotion by a person. Fear is studied as the effects of stimuli that precede aversive stimuli — a situation in which we would agree with the person, hence reinforcing his response, if he said he were afraid. This does not, of course, guarantee that the emotion itself will always be the same in each organism experiencing the same conditions or even in the same organism from exposure to exposure to the pre-aversive stimuli. However, variability may occur with all emotions, as was seen in the account of the way in which the names of the emotions are learned. Defining an emotion in terms of the environmental circumstances — which are observable to all, including the person experiencing the emotion — is at least as valid as defining it in terms of descriptive behavior of the person or the constellation of internal behaviors he may happen to exhibit.

The Definition of Emotions

The early students of behavior believed that emotions were elicited by particular generic stimuli in human infants. Fear was thought to be elicited by a loud noise or loss of support, anger by restraint, and love by appropriate and gentle tactual stimulation of the body. While there are reliable correlations between such stimuli and the elicitation of the emotion in young children, the general cases seem to be a little more complicated. Fear and anxiety are studied today as the effects of aversive stimuli and of the conditioned aversive stimuli that precede the aversive stimuli. Hate, anger, and aggressiveness are, at least in part, studied in terms of aggressive behavior elicited by aversive stimuli. The tender emotions are mostly neglected in research in experimental psychology because of their tenuousness and evanescence; but they seem to involve a change in the prevailing discriminative stimuli and conditioned reinforcers from those associated with less reinforcing conditions to those associated with more reinforcing conditions. In other words, they have to do with conditioned positive reinforcers rather than with conditioned aversive stimuli. The experimental study of emotion proceeds as an analysis of the effects on behavior of these generic environmental conditions.

What follows is a brief treatment of the characteristic methods of studying two well-defined emotions, fear and anger, and the results of such studies. The general considerations, however, are also pertinent to the analysis of the tender emotions.

Fear and Anxiety

Fear and anxiety, which need not be considered separately for our present purposes, are produced by aversive and conditioned aversive stimuli. Everyone knows from experience the manifestations of these two emotions in internal feelings, although probably no two individuals experience them in exactly the same way.

The Definition and Measurement of Anxiety

Anxiety is usually studied behaviorally as the effects of a conditioned aversive stimulus on operant behavior maintained by a schedule of positive reinforcement, typically a variable-interval schedule. This schedule provides a base-line of responding at a fairly constant rate, against which the effects of the conditioned aversive stimulus can be measured with accuracy. After the rate of responding has stabilized on the VI schedule, a neutral stimulus, such as a light, is introduced at variable intervals for a constant period of time, such as a minute or two. The light terminates with the presentation of an aversive stimulus, such as an electric shock or a loud noise, regardless of whether the organism is responding. After several presentations of the light followed by the aversive stimulus, the light becomes a conditioned aversive stimulus. The schedule of positive reinforcement continues without interruption during the conditioned stimulus. Thus, any changes in the positively reinforced behavior can be attributed to the conditioned aversive and the aversive stimuli.

The light has little effect on behavior when it is first introduced. Only after it takes on its conditioned aversive functions does it begin to influence responding. The first few presentations of the primary aversive stimulus, however, produce a subsequent disruption and suppression of the positively reinforced responding. Gradually, as the number of presentations of the aversive stimulus increases, the aftereffect of the aversive stimulus decreases, or habituates, and the conditioned aversive stimulus comes to suppress responding prior to the presentation of the primary aversive stimulus. The amount of suppression increases as the termination of the conditioned aversive stimulus, and hence the occurrence of the aversive stimulus, approaches. A very low rate of responding, usually zero, typically prevails during the fifteen to thirty seconds or so immediately preceding the aversive stimulus.

The amount of the suppression is conveniently expressed as the *suppression ratio:* the ratio of the rate prevailing during successive intervals of time during the presentation of the conditioned aversive stimulus to the rate prevailing in the absence of the conditioned aversive stimulus. The amount of suppression depends on a large number of variables, such as the intensity of the aversive stimulus, the duration of the conditioned aversive stimulus, the rate of reinforcement provided by the schedule, and the type of reinforcement schedule.

The suppression of responding is an effect of the conditioned aversive stimulus. It is not owing to extinction, since the schedule of positive reinforcement continues in effect; nor to punishment, since the aversive stimulus at least sometimes occurs in the absence of responding; nor to the aversive stimulus alone, since the suppression is nearly eliminated when the aversive stimulus is presented without a conditioned aversive stimulus.

The Control of Anxiety

Two methods of eliminating or attenuating the suppression of responding will be discussed here, since each of them suggests a possible way of controlling anxiety. The first method involves the use of avoidance training. After the conditioned aversive stimulus has come to suppress responding regularly and effectively, the organism is trained to avoid the aversive stimulus. The training is carried out in a different environment to minimize the effects of ordinary generalization, but the aversive stimulus is unchanged, and the response that avoids the aversive stimulus is the same as the response reinforced on the VI schedule. The response need not be shaped, since it is already in the organism's repertoire. Once avoidance has been established and maintained for a short time, the effect of the conditioned aversive stimulus in the original procedure is no longer to suppress responding but rather to facilitate it. Whether or not the organism still experiences anxiety is moot. The easily accessible components of the emotion are the emotion itself as validly as are the invisible, internal components. Regardless of the internal components, responding is no longer suppressed by the conditioned aversive stimulus. This sort of performance by a human organism in the presence of a conditioned aversive stimulus would have to be described as active attempts to cope with its environment.

The other method of reducing the amount of suppression involves the schedule of positive reinforcement that maintains the responding. Generally speaking, the conditioned aversive stimulus suppresses well-established responding on a moderate ratio schedule less than it suppresses responding on an interval schedule. Also, the amount of suppression is less when suppression would result in a substantial decrease in the frequency of positive reinforcement. Anxiety thus depends in part on the positively reinforcing maintenance conditions as well as on the character of the aversiveness responsible for the anxiety.

Hate, Anger, and Aggression

This second group of tough, as opposed to tender, emotions has recently been explored through studies of aggression. Aggression is a visible response, and it is defined, as are other responses, in terms of its effect on the environment. For this reason, it is difficult to define human aggression, since much of it is verbal.

The Definition and Measurement of Aggression

Animal aggression is easier to define since it usually involves biting or unusually violent contact with the environment. A common definition of aggression in animals is the closing of an electrical circuit via a closed air and mercury system that can be altered by constriction of one of its parts, a rubber tube. The rubber tube is usually constricted by biting, but the response class may include any other behavior that constricts the tube. This is an adequate definition of the aggressive response since it measures a class of behaviors similar to the class of aggressive behaviors that the organisms exhibit in their natural habitat and because the response behaves regularly as a function of its controlling variables.

Aggression is elicited by aversive stimuli. When an electric shock, for example, is presented to a rat, the rat will aggress against animate or inanimate objects in its immediately available environment. The object of aggression may be another organism of the same or different species or, when the rat is alone, the cage or the bars on the floor. If the rubber tube described above is available, the frequency, intensity, and persistence of the aggression can be measured. These variables depend on a number of factors, such as the frequency and intensity of the aversive stimulus.

It may turn out to be too broad a statement to say that all aversive stimuli elicit aggression, since there may yet turn out to be some that do not. Obviously, there will be conditions under which any given aversive stimulus will not elicit aggression. Nevertheless, the breadth of the statement gains some justification from the fact that aggression is elicited by stimuli associated with extinction, which, as we have seen in Chapter 9, can be shown to be aversive. It is also wise to hold open the possibility that other classes of stimuli besides the legitimately aversive may be elicitors of aggression, even though this does not seem plausible at present.

The Control of Aggression

Although the aggressive response is an elicited respondent when it first occurs, it has an operant aspect insofar as its frequency may be influenced by its consequences and insofar as it may be brought under the control of arbitrary stimuli. When the consequences of the aggressive response are reinforcing, as when fighting for food is reinforced by access to the food, the response develops an unusually high probability of occurrence and an elicitor of the aggressive response is then no longer required for its occurrence. If aggression is usually punished in the presence of one stimulus but is usually not punished or is reinforced in the presence of a second stimulus (the stimuli may be concurrent), then the differential consequences will bring the aggression under the control of the second stimulus.

These phenomena concern the operant aspect of the aggressive response, even though the response may be elicited by an aversive stimulus in a given instance. Every respondent involving the skeletal musculature probably has some operant aspect. An experimental analysis is necessary in each case to determine the relative contributions of each aspect to the occurrence of the behavior under a given set of circumstances.

THE RELATIONSHIP BETWEEN EMOTION AND MOTIVATION

Discussions of the relation of emotion to motivation traditionally begin with the observation that emotions are motivating. This is misleading because it allows confusion between motivation and reinforcement. The occurrence of some emotions and the termination of other emotions are reinforcing. However, that does not mean that it is correct to say that emotions are motivators, any more than it is correct to say that food is a motivator. Food is not a motivator; it is a reinforcer. Motivational variables, like deprivation, are what determine whether or not stimuli, such as food, will be effective as reinforcers at any given time.

A second source of ambiguity is that the same thing that produces an emotion may also create a motivational condition. An aversive stimulus both elicits aggression and provides the motivational condition for avoidance. The elicited aggression is not the motivation for avoidance. Moreover, if the aversive stimulus is of low intensity, the elicited aggression may habituate while the withdrawal of the aversive stimulus continues to maintain avoidance. There is no point in explaining one event in terms of another event if the first occurs in the absence of the second.

An emotion is motivational only if its occurrence is a necessary condition for a stimulus to be reinforcing or if the emotion increases the effectiveness of a reinforcer. For example, the aggressiveness elicited by an aversive stimulus is motivational insofar as it increases the effectiveness of the presentation of another organism as a reinforcer. Usually, although there are exceptions, an organism's behavior is reinforced by the presentation of another organism. When the organism is aggressive, however, the presentation of another organism, against whom the first organism aggresses, is more reinforcing; it will maintain a higher rate of responding. The presentation of another organism is not any more reinforcing than usual in cases where the aversive stimulus does not result in aggression against the second organism. Thus, the increase in reinforcing effectiveness is a motivational facet of aggression rather than a property of the aversive stimulus.

MOTIVATION IN OPERANT CONDITIONING

The distinctions that we have been making between motivational and other concepts may seem unduly tedious. However, they are essential for an understanding of behavior and for an adequate and useful technology of behavioral control.

Motivation as an explanatory and descriptive concept lost much of its usefulness during the historical transition from the view that reinforcement was associated primarily with the reduction of various drives and needs to the functional definition of reinforcement that is used in this primer—particularly as a result of the exploration of schedules of reinforcement and their powerful control over behavior. The practitioner of operant conditioning scarcely mentions motivation, since it has come to refer only to those conditions that render a given event reinforcing at a given time. Since the emphasis in operant conditioning is on the effects of reinforcement, these motivational conditions have become mere technological details. The pigeon, for example, is routinely maintained at eighty per cent of its free-feeding weight, because this is a sufficient motivational condition to render food reinforcing. The magnitude of the electric shock delivered to rats as the motivational condition for avoidance has likewise been standardized, within rather narrow limits, by the accumulated experience which makes up the technology of research. Only when a new species is approached must the motivational conditions be dealt with explicitly. As soon as the deprivation that renders food an effective reinforcer and the intensity of shock that maintains avoidance have been discovered, motivational considerations sneak quietly back into the role of established technological practice for the new organism. Research proceeds to the effects of the reinforcer which the motivational considerations make possible.

Concurrently, research attempts to answer the primary, legitimate motivational question: When and why is a reinforcer reinforcing? For the human organism, the problem is often complicated. The behavior of children, for example, may be reinforced by a variety of events, but the reinforcers generally share the troublesome property of evanescence. What is reinforcing at one moment may not be reinforcing a very short time later. It is a difficult, although empirical and solvable, problem to find motivational conditions under which reinforcers are not evanescent. Two practical solutions are to vary the reinforcer continually and to work with experimental sessions so short that evanescence cannot occur; but these merely by-pass the fundamental motivational problem.

Since all reinforcers, at first glance, seem to have in common only the property that they are functionally reinforcing, it is tempting to search for the why of reinforcement outside of the province of psychology. Usually a physiological answer is attempted. Do reinforcers reinforce because they all produce a certain electrical spectrum in a certain set of structures in the central nervous system? Is their final nervous effect the common element shared by light for an animal maintained in darkness, by food for a hungry animal, and by a brilliantly executed cadenza for the person who goes to concerts? No answer is currently available, and none may ever be. But such questions as these are not psychological. The science of behavior—the understanding, prediction, and control of behavior—can continue to function, develop, and flourish as it has in the past without appealing to physiological fantasies about the communality of reinforcers.

The fundamental, psychological question remains, despite appeals to other sciences for aid. The question of when and why a reinforcer is reinforcing has a deceptively easy answer in the case of animals reinforced with food. Food is a reinforcer when the organism has been sufficiently deprived of food and also when the organism has been exposed to certain training procedures. Another way of stating this, which leads to a statement of apparently considerable generality, is that food will serve as a reinforcer if the organism has been made, by deprivation or training, highly likely to eat in the presence of food. In general, events and activities will be reinforcers when the organism has a high probability of engaging in certain behaviors in their presence. This turns out to be a highly productive way of examining reinforcers. For example, it can be shown that organisms deprived of water will run in order to receive an opportunity to drink. This is not surprising. What is surprising, however, is that animals deprived of exercise will drink in order to receive an opportunity to run. The principle uniting these two effects seems to be that the opportunity to engage in behavior which is currently highly probable is reinforcing. The most attractive aspect of this approach to the fundamental motivational problem, as stated above, is that it offers an answer to the question in a purely psychological context, without appealing to other areas of investigation.

This represents the proper evolution of the science of behavior. In its history as a concept, motivation has often been so abused and overextended that its use verged on the meaningless. Explanations of behavior in motivational terms came to sound as hollow as the obviously spurious comment that the chicken doesn't cross the road because it doesn't want to. Retrenchment was called for and, fortunately, took place. The *ad hoc, post hoc* postulation of seemingly reasonable reasons for behavior slowly gave way to a sober, operational view of motivation, a view that finds motivation of surprisingly little usefulness in the analysis and control of behavior. This is certainly not to say that there are no important and legitimately motivational problems; but it does point out that many of the phenomena naïvely labeled motivational have shown themselves, under the experimental analysis of behavior, to be phenomena whose relevant controlling variables are in an entirely different domain.

For example, the problem of inaction in a particular situation is commonly explained as a lack of motivation: If the organism were motivated, it would behave and, moreover, would behave correctly (if, of course, the motivation were not too great). This sort of explanation does no more than give a common-sense reason for the occurrence or nonoccurrence of behavior. It gives no indication of the controlling variables. It is thus inherently useless. Moreover, it may be in error. If the inaction is occasioned by the early part of a fixed-interval schedule of reinforcement, it is incorrect to attribute it to a lack of motivation.

The most serious and sorrowful of the difficulties raised by motivational explanations is that they are misleading in terms of what procedures should be followed to alter the behavior. Suppose that the inaction is occasioned by the schedule of reinforcement. A motivational explanation suggests that the inaction would be abolished by an increase in motivation. This is simply not true with the fixed-interval schedule, since the control of the behavior in the early part of the interval is resistant to changes in motivation. Increased motivation does not produce high rates of responding soon after reinforcement. The problem is that the organism has recently been exposed to a discriminative stimulus (the previous reinforcement) associated with extinction. It can be solved only by changing the schedule of reinforcement to one in which responding is reinforced in the presence of the discriminative stimulus that currently occasions no responding. This may be accomplished with a variable-interval schedule that occasionally provides a very short period of time between two successive reinforcements. This schedule produces responding soon after reinforcement. The point is that such problems are questions of reinforcement and discriminative stimuli and not questions of motivation. The solution to problems of behavioral alteration and control, not to mention the understanding of such problems, lies primarily in a careful explication of the reinforcement dependencies and contingencies that currently bear on the organism's behavior. Motivational considerations turn out to be of extremely little importance.

Motivational concepts were essential to the description and analysis of behavior when the other available concepts were limited by the conception of a rigid, one-to-one connection between the stimulus and the response. Such a view relegated operant behavior to the level of reflexive, respondent behavior. With such a poverty of concepts, motivational considerations were needed not only to lend appeal to the explanations of behavior but also to make them even a little plausible.

The notion of a rigid bond between stimulus and response, however, has slowly vanished. It has been replaced by the protean and subtle processes inherent in the notions of the arbitrariness of the stimulus and the response, both conceived of as functionally defined classes of events; in the notion of the contingencies and dependencies arranged by the prevailing schedules of reinforcement;

and in the notion of a probability of emission of the response in the presence of a given set of discriminative stimuli. Armed with these powerful concepts, operant conditioning has found motivational conceptions of the will or of other states or drives of the organism to be unnecessary in accounting for, controlling, and understanding the behavior of organisms.

Selected Supplementary Readings

Further study of operant conditioning should include a reading of B. F. Skinner's *The Behavior of Organisms* (New York: Appleton-Century-Crofts, 1938) and his *Verbal Behavior* (New York: Appleton-Century-Crofts, 1957). Compendious information on many schedules of reinforcement is found in C. B. Ferster and B. F. Skinner, *Schedules of Reinforcement* (New York: Appleton-Century-Crofts, 1957). In addition, a variety of topics, both historical and contemporary, are treated in two collections of readings: B. F. Skinner (Ed.), *Cumulative Record* (New York: Appleton-Century-Crofts, 1961, enlarged edition) and A. C. Catania (Ed.), *Contemporary Research in Operant Behavior* (Glenview, Ill.: Scott, Foresman and Company, 1968).

The following references, grouped by chapter, have proved particularly useful to this author's students in furthering their detailed knowledge of the principles and facts of operant conditioning. While any listing of contributions to operant conditioning must be incomplete and somewhat arbitrary, it is hoped that the following selections will assist the reader in beginning a more detailed study.

One: INTRODUCTION TO THE EXPERIMENTAL
ANALYSIS OF BEHAVIOR

The theoretical, philosophical, and empirical foundations of operant conditioning are well represented in three papers by B. F. Skinner: "A case history in scientific method," *Amer. Psychologist*, 1956, *11*, 221-233; Are theories of learning necessary?, *Psychol. Rev.*, 1950, *57*, 193-216; and Freedom and the control of men, *Amer. Scholar*, Winter, 1955-1956, *25* (Special Issue), 47-65. The breadth of the system is documented by M. Sidman, Normal sources of pathological behavior, *Science*, 1960, *130*, 61-68.

Two: RESEARCH IN OPERANT CONDITIONING

Research in operant conditioning is further characterized in the introduction to *Schedules of Reinforcement*; in C. B. Ferster, The use of the free operant in the analysis of behavior, *Psychol. Bull.*, 1953, *50*, 263-274; and in B. F. Skinner, H. C. Solomon, and O. R. Lindsley, A new method for the experimental analysis of the behavior of psychotic patients, *J. nerv. ment. Dis.*, 1964, *120*, 403-406.

Three: ACQUISITION AND EXTINCTION
OF OPERANT BEHAVIOR

The acquisition and extinction of operant behavior is treated in considerable detail in *The Behavior of Organisms.* Of particular educational value also are the following papers: B. F. Skinner, On the rate of formation of a conditioned reflex, *J. gen. Psychol.*, 1932, *7*, 274-286; B. F. Skinner, "Superstition" in the pigeon, *J. exper. Psychol.*, 1948, *38*, 168-172; J. M. Notterman, Force emission during bar pressing, *J. exper. Psychol.*, 1959, *58*, 341-347; J. J. Antonitis, Response variability in the white rat during conditioning, extinction, and reconditioning, *J. exper. Psychol.*, 1951, *42*, 273-281; E. Hearst, Resistance-to-extinction functions in the single organism, *J. exper. Anal. Behav.*, 1961, *4*, 133-144.

Four: STIMULUS CONTROL OF OPERANT BEHAVIOR

The diverse area of stimulus control may be approached through the relevant sections of *The Behavior of Organisms.* An illuminating description of generalization appears in D. Blough, The shape of some wavelength generalization gradients, *J. exp. Anal. Behav.*, 1961, *4*, 31-40. The dynamics of responding during the formation of a discrimination are discussed in G. S. Reynolds, Contrast, generalization, and the process of discrimination, *J. exp. Anal. Behav.*, 1961, *4*, 289-294, whose references provide additional reading. Further information on attention, generalization, and discrimination is found in H. M. Jenkins and R. H. Harrison, Effect of discrimination training on auditory generalization, *J. exp. Psychol.*, 1960, *59*, 246-253, and in G. S. Reynolds, Attention in the pigeon, *J. exp. Anal. Behav.*, 1961, *4*, 203-208. The intricacies of transferring discriminative control from one continuum to another are introduced in H. S. Terrace, Errorless transfer of a discrimination across two continua, *J. exp. Anal. Behav.*, 1963, *6*, 223-232. An analysis of temporal generalization and discrimination appears in G. S. Reynolds and A. C. Catania, Temporal discrimination in pigeons, *Science*, 1962, *135*, 314-315, and in G. S. Reynolds, Discrimination and emission of temporal intervals by pigeons, *J. exp. Anal. Behav.*, 1966, *9*, 65-68.

Five: CONDITIONED REINFORCERS

An excellent summary of conditioned reinforcement is contained in R. T. Kelleher and L. Gollub, A review of positive conditioned reinforcement, *J. exp. Anal. Behav.*, 1962, *5*, 543-597, and recent exciting advances in this area are explored in R. T. Kelleher, Conditioned reinforcement in second-order schedules, *J. exp. Anal. Behav.*, 1966, *9*, 475-486. A fundamental paper in the area of aversive stimulation is M. Sidman, By-products of aversive control, *J. exp. Anal. Behav.*, 1958, *1*, 265-280.

Six: SIMPLE SCHEDULES OF POSITIVE REINFORCEMENT

Schedules of Reinforcement contains a wealth of specific information relevant to this area. An instructive analysis of the performance maintained by interval schedules of reinforcement is approached in A. C. Catania and G. S. Reynolds, A quantitative analysis of the responding maintained by interval schedules of reinforcement, *J. exp. Anal. Behav.*, suppl., May 1968. The analysis of performance in terms of interresponse times that was begun in *The Behavior of Organisms* is treated in some depth in D. Anger, The dependence of interresponse times upon the relative reinforcement of different interresponse times, *J. exp. Psychol.*, 1956, *52*, 145-161, and in C. P. Shimp, The reinforcement of short interresponse times, *J. exp. Anal. Behav.*, 1967, *10*, 425-434. The effects of reinforcement schedules on behavior that is not directly reinforced are treated in B. F. Skinner and W. H. Morse, Concurrent activity under fixed-interval reinforcement, *J. comp. physiol. Psychol.*, 1957, *50*, 279-281, and in C. B. Ferster, Intermittant reinforcement of matching to sample in the pigeon, *J. exp. Anal. Behav.*, 1960, *3*, 259-272.

Seven: MULTIPLE COMPOUND, AND CONCURRENT SCHEDULES OF REINFORCEMENT

Schedules of Reinforcement also contains information on compound and complex schedules. Some of the events characterizing multiple schedules are discussed in G. S. Reynolds, An analysis of interactions in a multiple schedule, *J. exp. Anal. Behav.*, 1961, *4*, 107-117. A challenging analysis of the variables controlling performance under schedules of reinforcement is afforded by R. J. Herrnstein and W. H. Morse, A conjunctive schedule of reinforcement, *J. exp. Anal. Behav.*, 1958, *1*, 15-24. An introduction to concurrent scheduling is provided by two papers by R. J. Herrnstein: Some factors influencing behavior in a two-response situation, *Trans. N.Y. Acad. Sci.*, 21, *1*, 35-45, and Relative and absolute strength of response as a function of frequency of reinforcement, *J. exp. Anal. Behav.*, 1961, *4*, 262-272.

Eight: RESPONDENT BEHAVIOR AND RESPONDENT
CONDITIONING

The irreplaceable introduction to a detailed knowledge of respondent conditioning is I. P. Pavlov, *Conditioned Reflexes* (London: Oxford University Press, 1927). An experimental analysis of instinctive behavior appears in N. Peterson, Control of behavior by the presentation of an imprinted stimulus, *Science*, 1960, *132*, 1395-1396. Areas of current interest in respondent conditioning are described in K. Salzinger and M. B. Waller, The operant control of vocalization in the dog, *J. exp. Anal. Behav.*, 1962, *5*, 383-389, and in M. M. Shapiro, Respondent salivary conditioning during operant lever pressing in dogs, *Science*, 1960, *132*, 619-620.

Nine: AVERSIVE CONTROL: ESCAPE, AVOIDANCE,
AND PUNISHMENT

The source of reinforcement of avoidance is examined in the context of historical treatments of this subject by R. J. Herrnstein and P. M. Hineline, Negative reinforcement as shock-frequency reduction, *J. exp. Anal. Behav.*, 1966, *9*, 421-430. The character of M. Sidman's breakthrough into the modern study of avoidance is found in two of his papers, Two temporal parameters in the maintenance of avoidance behavior by the white rat, *J. comp. physiol. Psychol.*, 1953, *46*, 253-261, and Some properties of the warning stimulus in avoidance behavior, *J. comp. physiol. Psychol.*, 1955, *48*, 444-450, and in M. Sidman and J. J. Boren, The relative aversiveness of warning signal and shock in an avoidance situation, *J. abnorm. soc. Psychol.*, 1957, *55*, 339-344.

A good introduction to some of the variables involved in escape is J. A. Dinsmoor and E. Winograd, Shock intensity in variable interval escape schedules, *J. exp. Anal. Behav.*, 1958, *1*, 145-148.

The varied effects of punishment on behavior have been reviewed by R. M. Church, *Psychol. Rev.*, 1963, *70*, 369-402. The modern reorientation to the problem of punishment can be found in two papers by W. C. Holz and N. H. Azrin: A comparison of several procedures for eliminating behavior, *J. exp. Anal. Behav.*, 1963, *6*, 399-406, and Discriminative properties of punishment, *J. exp. Anal. Behav.*, 1961, *4*, 225-232. The reader interested in aversive control should not miss reading R. T. Kelleher, W. C. Riddle, and L. Cook, Persistent behavior maintained by unavoidable shocks, *J. exp. Anal. Behav.*, 1963, *6*, 507-517. And further effects are discussed in C. B. Ferster, Control of behavior in chimpanzees and pigeons by time out from positive reinforcement, *Psychol. Monogr.*, 1958, *72*, Whole No. 461.

Ten: EMOTION AND MOTIVATION

The reader interested in the scientific study of emotion in operant conditioning should consult, by way of introduction, R. J. Herrnstein and M. Sidman, Avoidance conditioning as a factor in the effects of unavoidable shocks on food-reinforced behavior, *J. comp. physiol. Psychol.*, 1958, *51*, 380-385, and R. J. Herrnstein and W. H. Morse, Some effects of response-independent positive reinforcement on maintained operant behavior, *J. comp. physiol. Psychol.*, 1957, *50*, 461-467. Recent advances in the study of aggression are provided by N. H. Azrin and his co-workers: Extinction induced aggression, *J. exp. Anal. Behav.*, 1966, *9*, 191-204, and The opportunity for aggression as an operant reinforcer during aversive stimulation, *J. exp. Anal. Behav.*, 1965, *8*, 171-180.

The notions underlying the behavioral approach to the basis of reinforcement are introduced in two papers by D. Premack: Toward empirical behavioral laws: I. Positive reinforcement, *Psychol. Rev.*, 1959, *66*, 219-233, and Reversibility of the reinforcement relation, *Science*, 1962, *136*, 255-257.

In addition to these selected references, the reader can find access to the literature on the topics discussed here through the excellent index volumes of the *Journal of the Experimental Analysis of Behavior.*

Index